A Treasury of
New Zealand Verse

Being a New Edition of
"New Zealand Verse"

BY

W. F. Alexander *and* A. E. Currie.

WHITCOMBE AND TOMBS LIMITED

Auckland Christchurch Dunedin and Wellington N.Z.
Melbourne and London

Preface to Second Edition.

This work is a revised and enlarged edition of *New Zealand Verse*, published in 1906, and now out of print. To the original collection forty-three new pieces have been added, some the more recent work of contributors represented in the first edition, the rest selected from eighteen new contributors. Exigencies of space have entailed the omission of a number of other newer writers, and the excision of twenty-four of the pieces previously included. Thanks are due to the authors whose assistance has enabled the work to be brought in some measure up to date, and, it is hoped, made not less representative of the full body of New Zealand verse than was the first edition twenty years ago. Acknowledgment is also made to the publishers of books of verse and periodicals, enumerated elsewhere, who have given permission to republish verse of which they hold the copyright.

W. F. A.
A. E. C.

April, 1926.

1074.

CONTENTS

A TREASURY OF
NEW ZEALAND VERSE

New Zealand.

GOD girt her about with the surges,
   And winds of the masterless deep,
With tumult that rouses and urges
   Quick billows to sparkle and leap ;
He filled from the life of their motion
   Her nostrils with breath of the sea
And gave her afar in the ocean
   A citadel free.

Her never the fever-mists shrouding
   Nor blasts of the desert-wind blight,
Nor pall of drear smoke overclouding
   Toil's merciless cities of night,
But her Sun-God wings shafts from his quiver
   Over hills that are pasturelands fair
By shores where each league hath its river
   And life thrills the air.

Her beauty abides in all changes
   O'er isles where the palm meets the pine,
Where torrents sweep cold from white ranges
   To coasts of the fern-tree and vine,
Till the voices of streams that rushed waking
   The gorges hoarse cataracts fill
Are lost in the roar of seas breaking,
   The sound never still.

Her youth is made heir of the ages,
   Her children are freemen and peers,
Plain workers, yet sure of the wages
   Slow destiny pays with the years ;
Though little and latest their nation,
   Yet this they have won without sword,
That woman with man shall have station,
   The toiler be lord.

Not multitudes starving and striving,
   Not bondmen of misery's dearth,
But builders with patience contriving
   A kindlier realm upon earth,
Where pity worn age shall environ
   Where the young start abreast in their race,
Nor shall Fate with a gauntlet of iron
   Smite Poverty's face !

Peaks piercing the silence of heaven,
   Snows gleaming in luminous space,
See her waves round a hemisphere driven
   Fling their crests to the winds as they race ;
And the stars watch her lamp newly lighted
   And its beams shot afar o'er the sea
With a light of old wrongs at length righted
   By men who are free.

William Pember Reeves.

II.

To One in England.

I SEND to you
Songs of a Southern Isle,
Isle like a flower
In warm seas low lying :
   Songs to beguile
Some wearisome hour,
When Time's tired of flying.

Songs which were sung
To a rapt listener lying,
In sweet lazy hours,
Where wild-birds' nests swung,
And winds came a-sighing
In Nature's own bowers.

Songs which trees sung,
By summer winds swayed
Into rhythmical sound ;
Sweet soul-bells rung
Through the ngaio's green shade,
Unto one on the ground.

   Songs from an island
Just waking from sleeping
In history's morning ;
Songs from a land
Where night shadows creep
When your day is dawning.

O songs, go your way,
Over seas, over lands ;
Though friendless betimes,
Fear not, comes a day
When the world will clasp hands
With my wandering rhymes.

Eleanor Elizabeth Montgomery.

III.

The Night-watch Song of the "Charlotte Jane."

'Tis the first watch of the night, brothers,
    And the strong wind rides the deep ;
And the cold stars shining bright, brothers,
    Their mystic courses keep.
Whilst our ship her path is cleaving
    The flashing waters through,
Here's a health to the land we are leaving,
    And the land we are going to !

First sadly bow the head, brothers,
    In silence o'er the wine,
To the memory of the dead, brothers,
    The fathers of our line.
Though their tombs may not receive us,
    Far o'er the ocean blue,
Their spirits ne'er shall leave us,
    In the land we are going to.

Whilst yet sad memories move us,
  A second cup we'll drain
To the manly hearts that love us
  In our old homes o'er the main.
Fond arms that used to caress us,
  Sweet smiles from eyes of blue,
Lips which no more may bless us,
  In the land we are going to.

But away with sorrow now, brothers,
  Fill the wine-cup to the brim !
Here's to all who'll swear the vow, brothers,
  Of this our midnight hymn :
That each man shall be a brother,
  Who has joined our gallant crew ;
That we'll stand by one another
  In the land we are going to !

Fill again, before we part, brothers,
  Fill the deepest draught of all,
To the loved ones of our hearts, brothers,
  Who reward and share our toil.
From husbands and from brothers,
  All honour be their due,—
The noble maids and mothers
  Of the land we are going to !

The wine is at an end, brothers ;
  But ere we close our eyes,
Let a silent prayer ascend, brothers,
  For our gallant enterprise—

Should our toil be all unblest, brothers,
   Should ill winds of fortune blow,
May we find God's haven of rest, brothers,
   In the land we are going to.

James Edward FitzGerald.

IV.

The Old Year and the New.

WE beheld the old year dying
   In the country of our birth ;
When the drifted snow was lying
   On the hard and frozen earth.

Where the love of home was round us,
   By the blazing Christmas fires ;
And the love of country bound us
   To the hearthstones of our sires.

But our sons will see the glory
   Of the young and springing year ;
Where the green earth tells the story
   Of a younger hemisphere.

And the eve will lose its sadness
   In the hopefulness of day,—
In a birth so full of gladness,—
   In a death without decay.

But for us the morning's garland
   Glistens still with evening's dew ;—
We—the children of a far land,
   And the fathers of a new.

For we still, through old affection,
    Hear the old year's dying sigh,
Through the sad sweet recollection
    Of the years that are gone by.

While, through all the future gleaming,
    A bright golden promise runs,
And its happy light is streaming
    Of the greatness of our sons.

Pray we, then, whate'er betide them—
    Howsoever great they're grown—
That the past of England guide them,
    While the present is their own !

Charles C. Bowen.

v.

The Battle of the Free.

    To arms !   To arms !
  Hear ye not the trumpet's peal ?
  Hear ye not the clash of steel,—
And the sound of gathering armies in the Island of the
    Sea ?
Hear ye not the voice that calls them to the Battle of
    the Free ?
'Tis the voice of England calling on the free-born and
    the brave
To defend the lands of Freedom from the tyrant and
    the slave.

This is why her navies ride
On the gloomy northern tide ;
This is why her cannons roar
On the distant Euxine shore,
And her children haste away
To mingle in the bloody fray.
No lingering or debating till the deadly fight be won.
The maiden sends her lover,—and the mother sends
her son.
They are gathering, they are gathering, from the moun-
tain and the lea,
To rally round the banner of the Island of the Free.
Old England's arms are ringing
In hamlet and in hall,
And her sons, the sons of freedom,
Are coming at her call !
They are coming — they are coming—
To upraise the banner of the Island of the Sea,
And to fight in the Battle of the Free.

To arms !   To arms !
What are they, those glittering hosts,
Gathering on the neighbouring coasts
That look out on the waters of the Island of the Free ?
See ! their Eagles are mingled with the banners of the
sea,
And their joyous shout of greeting comes wafted unto
thee.
England ! where yon Eagles glance
Stands the chivalry of France !
Oh, England ! ne'er on battle plain
Shalt thou meet such foes again.

These are they who oft have tried
Thy mettle in the battle's tide ;
These are they whose Eagles flew
O'er the plain of Waterloo ;
Whose unsurrendering warriors fell
To shield the chief they loved so well.
  England, exult !
For thine ancient enemy is gathering unto thee,
To fight with thy children in the Battle of the Free.
  Oh, England ! those whose courage
    Thy fathers oft have tried ;—
  The French—thine ancient foemen,
    Will battle at thy side.
  They are coming—they are coming—
    To mingle their Eagles with the banners of the sea,
    And to fight in the Battle of the Free.

  To arms !   To arms !
    When Barbarian Armies roll,
    Countless, from the Northern pole,
To battle with the Eagle and the Lion of the Sea ;
When the deadly fight is raging,—the death fight that
    must be,
Between Liberty and Serfdom, ere the nations shall be
    free,—
When the shattered failing peoples look with trembling
    hope to thee :
Then, England, call thy children forth,
From East and West, and South and North,—
From every land of free-born men
Where thou hast planted liberty ;—
Oh, England ! call thy children then,
  And they will gladly answer thee.

Hark ! to the shores of the Island of the Free,
Their answer cometh floating o'er the voiceful sea !
   England, exult !
For thy numberless sons are gathering unto thee.
  Oh, England ! bear thee proudly
   In the direst need of war !
  Thy sons,—the sons of Freedom,—
   Are sailing from afar.
  They are coming—they are coming—
  To carry the banners of the Island of the Sea,
   And to fight in the Battle of the Free.

   To arms ! To arms !
  Echoes from the Western glades,—
  Echoes from the forest shades
Are flinging back their answer to the Island of the Sea,
Where her children are arming for the Battle of the Free.
They have heard the din of battle that comes wafted on
  the breeze,
In the sighing and the moaning of the tall dark forest
  trees ;
And their souls are stirred within them, and their homes
  have lost their charms,
When the Fatherland is calling all its chivalry to arms.
  To arms ! To arms ! the axe is ringing
   In the dark primeval wood,
  And a new-born forest springing
   On St. Lawrence's kingly flood.
A noble foliage on its boughs the parent forest bore,
Whence yon tapering mast was taken on the green
  Canadian shore ;
But it bears a nobler burden now, as yon navy sweeps
  to sea,—

For it bears the cross of England—the banner of the
    Free !

    Oh, England, send thy navies—
      Send them fearless to the war,
    For thy sons,—the gallant sailors,
      Are coming from afar.
    They are coming—they are coming—
To guard the waters of the Island of the Sea,
    And to fight in the Battle of the Free.

      To arms !   To arms !
    Hark ! what tramping hoofs resound
    On the glassy slopes around
The many-masted seaports of the Island of the Free.
What is this gathering of horses that I see ?
Those riderless horses from the park and from the lea ?
      England, exult !
For their horseless riders are coming o'er the sea.

    In their wild far-distant home
    They have heard thy call and come,
    With red spurs and loosened reins,
    Sweeping o'er Australia's plains.

They have left their reeking steeds on the wide Pacific's
    shore,
Whose wild waves rolling surdly the sounds of battle
    bore,
The drum-beat, and the shouting, and the cannon's
    angry roar ;
And ever through their music the gallant tidings ran
Of the rugged heights of Alma and the glens of Inker-
    mann.

Oh, England, land of horsemen !
　　Bring thy noblest steeds of war
For thy sons, the gallant riders,
　　Who are sailing from afar.
They are coming—they are coming—
To bestride the horses of the Island of the Sea,
And to fight in the Battle of the Free.

　　　To arms !　To arms !
　　When the battle rages fierce,
　　And the deadly volleys pierce
The small outnumbered army of the Island of the
　　Free ;—
When her dauntless hearts have chosen either death
　　or victory ;—
Where her warriors are fighting, as the bravest only dare,
For the birthplaces of freedom and the liberties of
　　man ;—

　　　Then New Zealand shall be there,
　　　　In the van.
　　　Young New Zealand shall be there,—
Her rifles from the mountain and her horsemen from
　　the plain
When the foemen's ranks are reeling o'er the slain.
　　　Few in number—stout of heart—
　　　They will come to take their part
In the dangers and the glories of the brave,
To share in their triumph or their blood-stained grave.

　　　　England, exult !
For thy numberless sons are coming o'er the sea,
To rally round the banner of the Island of the Free.

Oh, England ! bear thee proudly
  In the direst need of war ;
For thy sons,—the sons of Freedom,
  Are sailing from afar.
They are coming—they are coming—
To surround the banner of the Island of the Sea,
And to fight in the Battle of the Free.

Charles C. Bowen.

VI.

Early Days.

WANT to hear a story ? Want to come on Granny's
  knee ?
None the better for that party and the pastry, I can
  see !
Tired of all your dollies, and the picture-books ?
  Well, well !
I don't think *we'd* have tired....Now, you listen,
  and I'll tell.

....Once, there was a blue Bay—years and years
  ago ;—
Cramm'd with red and black pine, thick as they could
  grow ;
Half-a-dozen settlers, with as many children each ;
Not a track to anywhere, and Bush to the beach.

We'd no mail, or schoolhouse ; there was neither
  church nor store ;
People lived in pine-wood *wharés*, with pine-sawdust
  on the floor.

Strangers never came our way, playthings mostly grew,
An' Town might have been at Home, for all us young
    ones knew.

Always dress'd in dungaree : never had new boots !
Lived on pig and pigeon, *kaka*, fish, and roots.
But, chew, an' get the full good out of everything
    you've got,
And I guess you're just as well-off with a little as a lot.

Ay, sunshine : sunshine : freedom, an' content :
Bless those bare old Bay days—light enough they went !
—But what I was going to tell you, was, when Father's
    boat came down
After taking up the timber from the sawpit into Town.

Mother and Aunt was timid when the men-folk were
    away ;
Used to call us young ones in at dimming of the day.
We'd fetch in water and wood, and we'd make the
    wharé fast,
Snuggle under the blankets, an' wish the night was past.

But sometimes, sometimes ! in the middle of the night,
Round the Northern Head 'ud steal a little lonely light.
" *Coo-ee !* " 'd come the cry....Waken all ! and
    hark !....
Oh, it's father ! Father coming in the deadness of
    the Dark !

Then, one 'ud shift the back-log, for the hot red beneath,
One 'ud pile the kindling on, and blow with all her
    breath,
An', wide on the dreadful Dark, an' creepy, curdly Cold,
One 'ud run and fling the door, an' nobody 'ud scold !

" *Coo-ee*....*Coo-ee !* "....closer 'd come the sound....
Peer an' peer....at last we'd hear her being run
 aground !
Footsteps up the shingle !   Shout !....and answering
 shout !
Out we'd run an' pull 'em in, an' shut the Darkness out !

Father, Uncle Eb, an' big brother Dave—
Oh, so wet an' salty !   Oh, so big and brave !
Good it was to hug them, an' warm their wintry
 cheeks—
Sometimes they'd been up in Town, weather-bound
 for weeks.

Then I'd be at the bellows, an' I'd blow, blow, blow,
Till the brown walls were ruddy, an' the *wharé* all
 a-glow.
Merrily danced the fire-flicker, bright the flashes
 danced,
Upon merry heart-lit faces, an' bright eyes that danced.

Then Father'd weigh the baby, and declare we all
 were grown ;
Or he'd want the dimples counted, an' the last new
 freckles shown.
While close we'd cling about him, an' fossick in his
 coat—
" Lollies for the kiddies," always came in Father's
 boat.

Next, he'd toss the parcel Mother always caught :
Something tasty out o' Town, down for supper brought.
Hiss !   Splut !   Splutter !....Tending it in turn,
You can guess us children never let *that* cooking burn !

Meanwhile, the grown-ups 'ud be carrying in the swags ;
There'd be diving into bundles, an' dipping into bags. .
Matches : molasses : cotton, and salt an' such—
Puzzled me how Town got on, when the Bay had took
    so much ?

An', all the while, they'd tell us tales—what the timber
    brought,
Town-news, war-news, an' what vessels lay in port ;
An', Oh ! the people, an' places, an' sights an' all,
    they'd name—
How big ! how wonderful an' strange !—how *full* the
    world became !

An' sometimes, Oh ! a letter.—Then, 'twas " Get the
    slush-lamp, quick ! "
('Twas a hollow'd raw potato, stuff'd with stocking
    round a stick,
An' stuck, swamp'd with porpoise-oil, in a pannikin—
Smelt, Uncle used to say, worse than home-made sin);

An' then we'd hush an' settle down quiet round the
    hearth,
For to hear o' green Kent country, an' the old side
    of the Earth.
Uncle listen'd interested, Father with a frown ;
Mother used to listen with her head bow'd down.

It was always full o' stories ; folks were wedded,
    buried, born ;
There were animals, an' railways, an' " the cherries,"
    or " the corn."
All our plays 'ud be for days what the news had been ;—
An' 'twas nice that people loved you that you hadn't
    ever seen.

Well, an' after that, came Supper—for us young ones,
    too ; at least,
Mother'd let us have a taste, just to *feel* the feast.
An' wasn't she a picture ! pouring, good an' hot,
Tea (not *manuka*-brew, but Tea !) from the pot.

Then, amid the cosy, warm tobacco-smoke,
Through the deep, protecting tones of the men-folk,
Good it was to listen, with your head on Father's knee,
To the falling, lifting, falling, of the Sea !

Or, gazing through the window that look'd upon the
    tide,
To *dare* all that big, black, bogey Dark outside....
Outside, the pouncing Dark, and cold, cold foam,—
Inside, all of us—and Father ! safe back home.

Then, when all was over, all the good-nights said,
Fire cover'd up again, and every one in bed—
Why, bless me, child, 'twasn't over ! 'Tisn't yet—the
    dear delight
Of those sudden riches rain'd down in the middle of
    the night.

                   B. E. Baughan.

VII.

The First News frae Auld Scotland.

HAME letters !   I doubt there'll be nane for me ;
  This lang time past they hae been gey few ;
Nae monie are left sud muckle care
  To write the feckless auld man noo.
Thar's monie a change gane owre my head,
  That is unco careworn noo, and grey ;
An' monie a change owre the guid auld hame,
  Sin' sae weary I watch'd, the leelang day,
    For the first news frae Auld Scotland.

We were first to hae trod on these alien shores ;
  An' the hame-scenes cam' freshly in ilka e'e,
Where we wandered sae aft wi' the dear anes gane,
  An' the blue heather-bells bloom'd bonnilie ;
Ilk heart was fu' o' the auld lang syne,
  An' the hearty cheerin' went brawly roun',
As we watched the vessel outowre the sea—
  Tho' but unco slowly—come sailing down
    Wi' the first news frae Auld Scotland.

I mind as weel's it were but noo,
  How I graspit ilk hand as it were my fier's ;
For it seem'd to me they had come straight out
  Frae those I had left on the Greenock piers :
But wha, of a' that I kenn'd sae weel,
  Will gie a thought to the auld man noo ?
For monie are dead, and mair are chang'd,
  Sin' I welcom'd sae leal the lang-sought crew,
    Wi' the first news frae Auld Scotland.

I hae made me a hame i' the stranger lan' ;
  I hae gathered roun' me hearts couthie and true ;
And Otago's bonnie banks and braes
  Hae heartfelt ties to bind me noo ;
Yet weel I ken they maun haud for me,
  Nae memories sae leesome as cam' to me then,
Owre the braid, braid seas frae my native land,
  As I heard frae the lips o' my countrymen
    The first news frae Auld Scotland.

Catherine H. Richardson.

VIII.

For Love of Appin.

THE hand is to the plough an' the e'e is to the trail ;
The river-boatie dances wi' her heid to the gale ;
        But she'll never ride to Appin ;
        We'll see nae mair o' Appin ;
For ye ken we crooned " Lochaber " at the saut sea's
    gate.
        It's a land of giantrie ;
        Its lochs are like the sea.
        But it's no a desert fairly,
        The corn's fu' an' early ;
        Ye'll hear the laddies daffing ;
        Ye'll hear the lasses laughing ;
        But we—we canna tine
        What lies ayont the brine :

When we sang " Lochaber " then,
We were grey, grey men.
We'll smile nae mair for ever
By the prairie or the river,
Lest ony think perchance that we forget
The rainy road to Appin,—
East awa' to Appin,—
The rainy road to Appin that the leal men went.

They tore us out o' Scotland, they flang us in the west
Like a bairn's thread o' beads, an' we downa look for
rest.
But it's O to lie in Appin,—
I' the haly sod o' Appin,—
It's O to lie in Appin where the mist haps a' !
Cauld is this to live or die on,
But we brought the tents o' Zion ;
An' weel the mark is seen
Where the martyr-blood hath been
That will clear us to the Lord
When the Angel wi' the sword
Gangs nightly up the land
O' an Egypt that is banned.
But God do sae an' mair
To us, gin we cast a care,
Or smile again for ever
By the prairie or the river,
Lest ony think perchance that we forget
The red road to Appin,—
East awa' to Appin,—
The red road to Appin that the heart's blood tracked !

It's no a desert fairly, it's grand an' young an' fine :
Here the sons o' Anak might live an' press the wine :
   But it's O for hame an' Appin !—
   The heather hills o' Appin !—
The thousand years o' Appin where the leal men lie !
   Our face is set as stane,
   But we'll thank the Lord again,—
   Gang saftly a' our days ;
   An' wark shall be our praise.
   The bairns will tak' a root
   By the mighty mountain foot ;
   But we, we canna sever ;
   It's no for us whatever ;
   We hear nae earthly singing
   But it sets " Lochaber " ringing.
   An' we'll never smile again
   I' the sunlight or the rain
Till our feet are on the lang last trail,—
   The siller road to Appin,—
   East awa' to Appin,—
The siller road to Appin rinnin' a' the way to God !

       Jessie Mackay.

      IX.

The Dwellings of Our Dead.

THEY lie unwatched, in waste and vacant places,
In sombre bush or wind-swept tussock spaces,
 Where seldom human tread
And never human trace is—
 The dwellings of our dead !

No insolence of stone is o'er them builded ;
By mockery of monuments unshielded,
  Far on the unfenced plain
Forgotten graves have yielded
  Earth to free earth again.

Above their crypts no air with incense reeling,
No chant of choir or sob of organ pealing ;
  But ever over them
The evening breezes kneeling
  Whisper a requiem.

For some the margeless plain where nó one passes,
Save when at morning far in misty masses
  The drifting flock appears.
Lo, here the greener grasses
  Glint like a stain of tears !

For some the quiet bush, shade-strewn and saddened,
Whereo'er the herald tui, morning-gladdened,
  Lone on his chosen tree,
With his new rapture maddened,
  Shouts incoherently.

For some the gully, where in whispers tender,
The flax-blades mourn and murmur, and the slender
  White ranks of toi go,
With drooping plumes of splendour,
  In pageantry of woe.

For some the common trench where, not all fameless,
They fighting fell who thought to tame the tameless,
  And won their barren crown ;
Where one grave holds them nameless—
  Brave white and braver brown.

But in their sleep, like troubled children turning,
A dream of mother-country in them burning,
  They whisper their despair,
And one vague, voiceless yearning
  Burdens the pausing air....

" *Unchanging here the drab year onward presses ;*
No Spring comes trysting here with new-loosed tresses,
  And never may the years
Win Autumn's sweet caresses—
  Her leaves that fall like tears.

And we would lie 'neath old-remembered beeches,
Where we could hear the voice of him who preaches
  And the deep organ's call,
While close about us reaches
  The cool, grey, lichened wall."

But they are ours, and jealously we hold them ;
Within our children's ranks we have enrolled them,
  And till all Time shall cease
Our brooding bush shall fold them
  In her broad-bosomed peace.

They came as lovers come, all else forsaking,
The bonds of home and kindred proudly breaking ;
  They lie in splendour lone—
The nation of their making
  Their everlasting throne !

                              Arthur H. Adams

From *Maoriland, and Other Verses*, by permission of
the Bulletin Newspaper Company, Limited.

X.

A Colonist in His Garden.

He reads a letter.

" DIM grows your face, and in my ears,
Filled with the tramp of hurrying years,
    Your voice dies, far apart.
Our shortening day draws in, alack !
Old Friend, ere darkness falls, turn back
    To England, life and art.

" Write not that you content can be,
Pent by that drear and shipless sea
    Round lonely islands rolled,
Isles nigh as empty as their deep,
Where men but talk of gold and sheep
    And think of sheep and gold.

" A land without a past ; a race
Set in the rut of commonplace ;
    Where Demos overfed
Allows no gulf, respects no height ;
And grace and colour, music, light,
    From sturdy scorn are fled.

" I'll draw you home.   Lo !   As I write
A flash—a swallow's arrow-flight !
    O'erhead the skylark's wings
Quiver with joy at winter's rout :
A gust of April from without
    Scents of the garden brings.

" The quickening turf is starred with gold ;
The orchard wall, rust-red and old,
    Glows in the sunlight long.
The very yew-tree warms to-day,
As the sundial, mossed and grey,
    Marks with a shadow strong.

" Tired of the bold aggressive New,
Say, will your eyes not joy to view,
    In a sedater clime,
How mellowing tones at leisure steal,
And age hath virtue scars to heal,
    And beauty weds grey Time ? "

He speaks.
Good wizard ! Thus he weaves his spell.
Yet, charm he twenty times as well,
    Me shall he never spur,
To seek again the old, green land,
That seems from far to stretch a hand
    To sons who dream of her.

For is my England there ?   Ah, no.
Gone is my England, long ago,
    Leaving me tender joys,
Sweet unforgotten fragrance, names
Of wrinkled men and grey-haired dames,
    To me still girls and boys.

With these in youth let memory stray
In pleasance green, where stern to-day
    Works Fancy no mischance.
Dear pleasance—let no light invade
Revealing ravage Time hath made
    Amid thy dim romance!

Here am I rooted.   Firm and fast
We men take root who face the blast,
    When to the desert come,
We stand where none before have stood
And braving tempest, drought and flood,
    Fight Nature for a home.

Now, when the fight is o'er, what man
What wrestler, who in manhood's span
    Hath won so stern a fall,
Who, matched against the desert's power,
Hath made the wilderness to flower,
    Can turn, forsaking all ?

Yet that my heart to England cleaves
This garden tells with blooms and leaves
    In old familiar throng,
And smells, sweet English, every one,
And English turf to tread upon,
    And English blackbird's song.

" No art ? "   Who serve an art more great
Than we, rough architects of State
    With the old Earth at strife ?
" No colour ? "   On the silent waste
In pigments not to be effaced,
    We paint the hues of life.

" A land without a past ? "   Nay, nay.
I saw it, forty years this day.
    —Nor man, nor beast, nor tree.
Wide, empty plains where shadows pass
Blown by the wind o'er whispering grass
    Whose sigh crept after me.

Now when at midnight round my doors
The gale through sheltering branches roars,
    What is it to the might
Of the mad gorge-wind that o'erthrew
My camp—the first I pitched—and blew
    Our tents into the night ?

Mine is the vista where the blue
And white-capped mountains close the view.
    Each tapering cypress there
At planting in these hands was borne,
Small, shivering seedlings and forlorn,
    When all the plain was bare !

Skies, without music, mute through time,
Now hear the skylark's rippling climb
    Challenge their loftier dome.
And hark !   A song of gardens floats,
Rills, gushes clear—the self-same notes
    Your thrushes flute at Home.

See, I have poured o'er plain and hill
Gold open-handed, wealth that will
    Win children's children's smiles,
—Autumnal glories, glowing leaves,
And aureate flowers, and warmth of sheaves,
    Mid weary pastoral miles.

Yonder my poplars, burning gold,
Flare in tall rows of torches bold,
    Spire beyond kindling spire.
Then raining gold round silver stem
Soft birches gleam.   Outflaming them
    My oaks take ruddier fire.

And with my flowers about her spread
(None brighter than her shining head),
   The lady of my close,
My daughter, walks in girlhood fair.
Friend, could I rear in England's air
   A sweeter English rose ?

William Pember Reeves.

XI.

A Leave-taking.

THE seamen shout once and together,
   The anchor breaks up from the ground,
And the ship's head swings to the weather,
   To the wind and the sea swings round :
With a clamour the great sail steadies,
   In extreme of a storm scarce furled ;
Already a short wake eddies,
   And a furrow is cleft and curled
     To the right and left.

About me, light-hearted or aching,
   " Good-bye ! " cry they all, taking hand—
What hand do I find worth taking ?
   What face as the face of the land ?
I will utter a farewell greater
   Than any of friends in ships—
I will leave on the forehead of Nature
   The seal of a kiss—let the lips
     Of a song do this.

We part from the earth, from our mother,
  Her bosom of milk and of sleep,
We deliver our lives to another,
  To cast them away or to keep.
Many-mooded and merciless daughter,
  Uncertain, strange, dangerous sea,
O tender and turbulent water !
  Make gentle thy strength, for in thee
    We put trust for a length.

Float out from the harbour and highland
  That hides all the region I know,
Let me look a last time on the island
  Well seen from the sea to the snow.
The lines of the ranges I follow,
  I travel the hills with my eyes,
For I know where they make a deep hollow,
  A valley of grass and the rise
    Of streams clearer than glass.

O what am I leaving behind me ?
  No sorrow with tears for its debt—
No face that shall follow and find me—
  No friend to recall and regret—
Thought shall raise up the ghosts of some faces,
  But not of the faces of men.
A voice out of fair forest places
  Shall haunt me and call me, as when
    I dwelt by them all.

Now my days leave the soft silent byway,
  And clothed in a various sort,
In iron or gold, on the highway
  New feet shall succeed, or stop short :

Shod hard these may be, or made splendid,
   Fair and many, or evil and few,
But the going of bare feet has ended,
   Of naked feet set in the new
      Meadow grass sweet and wet.

I will long for the ways of soft walking,
   Grown tired of the dust and the glare,
And mute in the midst of much talking,
   Will pine for the silences rare ;
Streets of peril and speech full of malice
   Will recall me the pastures and peace
Which gardened and guarded those valleys
   With grasses as high as the knees,
      Calm as high as the sky.

As the soul, were the body made regal,
   With pinions completed and light,
Majestic and swift as yon seagull,
   Even now would I take a quick flight,
And my spirit of singing deliver
   In the old hidden birthplace of song,
Sitting fast by the rapid young river
   With trees overarched, by no strong
      Sun or moon ever parched.

A singing place fitter than vessel
   Cold winds draw away to the sea,
Where many birds flutter and nestle
   And come near and wonder at me,
Where the bell-bird sets solitudes ringing :
   Many times I have heard and thrown down
My lyre in despair of all singing ;
   For things lovely what word is a crown
      Like the song of a bird ?

That haunt is too far for me wingless,
   And the hills of it sink out of sight,
Yet my thought were but broken and stringless,
   And the daylight of song were but night,
If I could not at will a winged dream let
   Lift me and take me and set
Me again by the trees and the streamlet ;
    These leagues make a wide water, yet
      The whole world shall not hide.

For the island secure in my spirit
   At ease on its own ocean rides,
And Memory, a ship sailing near it,
   Shall float in with favouring tides,
Shall enter the harbours and land me
   To visit the gorges and heights
Whose aspects seemed once to command me,
    As queens by their charms command knights,
      To achievements of arms.

And I will catch sight of their faces
   Through the dust of the lists and the din,
In the sword-lit and perilous places—
   Yea, whether I lose or I win,
I will look to them, all being over,
   Triumphant or trampled beneath,
I will turn to the isle like a lover,
    To her evergreen brakes for a wreath,
      For a tear to her lakes.

The last of her now is a brightening
   Far fire in the forested hills,
The breeze as the night nears is heightening,
   The cordage draws tighter and thrills,

Like a horse that is spurred by the rider,
  The great vessel quivers and quails,
And passes the billows beside her,
  The fair wind is strong in her sails,
    She is lifted along.

When the zone and the latitude changes
  A welcome of white cliffs shall be,
I shall cease to be sad for white ranges
  Now lost in the night and the sea :—
But dipped deep in their clear flowing rivers
  As a chalice my spirit shall weigh
With fair water that flickers and shivers,
  Held up to the strong, steady ray,
    To the sunlight of song.

Frederick Napier Broome.

XII.

Written in Australia.

THE wide sun stares without a cloud :
  Whipped by his glances truculent,
The earth lies quivering and cowed !
  My heart is hot with discontent—
  I hate this haggard continent.

  But over the loping leagues of sea
  A lone land calls to her children free ;
  My own land holding her arms to me
  Over the loping leagues of sea.

The old grey city is dumb with heat ;
   No breeze comes leaping, naked, rude,
Adown the narrow, high-walled street ;
   Upon the night thick perfumes brood :
   The evening oozes lassitude.

But o'er the edges of my town,
   Swept in a tide that ne'er abates,
The riotous breezes tumble down ;
   My heart looks home, looks home, where waits
   The Windy City of the Straits !

The land lies desolate and stripped ;
   Across its waste has thinly strayed
A tattered host of eucalypt,
   From whose gaunt uniform is made
   A ragged penury of shade.

But o'er my isles the forest drew
   A mantle thick—save where a peak
Shows his grim teeth a-snarl—and through
   The filtered coolness creek and creek
   Tangled in ferns, in whispers speak.

And there the placid great lakes are,
   And brimming rivers proudly force
Their ice-cold tides.   Here, like a scar,
   Dry-lipped, a withered watercourse
   Crawls from a long-forgotten source.

My glance, home-gazing, scarce discerns
   This listless girl, in whose dark hair
A starry-red hibiscus burns ;
   Her pallid cheeks are like a pair
   Of nuns—they are so fragile-fair ;

C

And like a sin her warm lips flame
   In her wan face ; swift passions brim
In her brown eyes, and ebb with shame ;
   Her form is sinuous and slim—
   That lyric line of breast and limb !

But one there waits whose brown face glows,
   Whose cheeks with Winter's kisses smart—
The flushing petals of a rose !
   Of earth and sun she is a part ;
   Her brow is Greek and Greek her heart.

At love she laughs a faint disdain ;
   Her heart no weakly one to charm ;
Robust and fragrant as the rain,
   The dark bush soothed her with his balm,
   The mountains gave her of their calm.

Her fresh young figure, lithe and tall,
   Her twilight eyes, her brow benign,
She is the peerless queen of all—
   The maid, the country, that I shrine
   In this far banished heart of mine !

     But over the loping leagues of green
     A lone land waits with a hope serene—
     My own land calls like a prisoner queen—
     But oh ! the long loping leagues between !

           Arthur H. Adams.

XIII.

In London.

WHEN I look out on London's teeming streets,
On grim grey houses, and on leaden skies,
My courage fails me, and my heart grows sick,
And I remember that fair heritage
Barter'd by me for what your London gives.
This is not Nature's city : I am kin
To whatsoever is of free and wild,
And here I pine between these narrow walls,
And London's smoke hides all the stars from me,
Light from mine eyes, and Heaven from my heart.

For in an island of those Southern seas
That lie behind me, guided by the Cross
That looks all night from out our splendid skies,
I know a valley opening to the East.
There, hour by hour, the lazy tide creeps in
Upon the sands I shall not pace again—
Save in a dream,—and, hour by hour, the tide
Creeps lazily out, and I behold it not,
Nor the young moon slow sinking to her rest
Behind the hills ; nor yet the dead white trees
Glimmering in the starlight : they are ghosts
Of what has been, and shall be never more.
No, never more !

Nor shall I hear again
The wind that rises at the dead of night
Suddenly, and sweeps inward from the sea,
Rustling the tussock, nor the wekas' wail
Echoing at evening from the tawny hills.

In that deserted garden that I lov'd,
Day after day, my flowers drop unseen ;
And as your Summer slips away in tears,
Spring wakes our lovely Lady of the Bush,
The Kowhai, and she hastes to wrap herself
All in a mantle wrought of living gold ;
Then come the birds, who are her worshippers,
To hover round her : tuis swift of wing,
And bell-birds flashing sudden in the sun,
Carolling : ah ! what English nightingale,
Heard in the stillness of a summer eve,
From out the shadow of historic elms,
Sings sweeter than our Bell-bird of the Bush ?
And Spring is here : now the Veronica,
Our Koromiko, whitens on the cliff,
The honey-sweet Manuka buds, and bursts
In bloom, and the divine Convolvulus,
Most fair and frail of all our forest flowers,
Stars every covert, running riotous.
O quiet valley, opening to the East,
How far from this thy peacefulness am I !
Ah me, how far ! and far this stream of Life
From thy clear creek fast falling to the sea !

Yet let me not lament that these things are
In that lov'd country I shall see no more ;
All that has been is mine inviolate,
Lock'd in the secret book of memory.
And though I change, my valley knows no change.
And when I look on London's teeming streets,
On grim grey houses, and on leaden skies,
When speech seems but the babble of a crowd,

And music fails me, and my lamp of life
Burns low, and Art, my mistress, turns from me,—
Then do I pass beyond the Gate of Dreams
Into my kingdom, walking unconstrained
By ways familiar under Southern skies ;
Nor unaccompanied ; the dear dumb things
I lov'd once, have their immortality.
There too is all fulfilment of desire :
In this the valley of my Paradise
I find again lost ideals, dreams too fair
For lasting ; there I meet once more mine own
Whom Death has stolen, or Life estranged from me ;
And thither, with the coming of the dark,
Thou comest, and the night is full of stars.

Dora Wilcox.

XIV.

The Man Away.

THEY marvelled that in lands so old
    He yet could dream of younger skies,
That he could still his heart withhold,
    Forbid content creep to his eyes.

Upon their wharfs 'mid masts and hulls,
    His thoughts like little waves would run,
Past Terawhiti's storm of gulls
    To Mana drowsing in the sun.

And from his attic, caring naught,
    He lured the birds unto his sills
Whose wings were nearer to his thought,
    For they had known the Southern hills.

For they had heard from golden tree
    With dripping beak a tui sing,
And learned with what wet mystery
    Manuka bloweth in the Spring.

And so he dreamed among the roofs,
    Kneading the world to singing words,
His lyre the beat of passing hoofs,
    His only friend the birds.

Eileen Duggan.

xv.

From " Ranolf and Amohia."

IT was a wondrous realm beguiled
Our youth amid its charms to roam ;
O'er scenes more fair, serenely wild,
Not often summer's glory smiled ;
When flecks of cloud, transparent, bright,
No alabaster half so white—
Hung lightly in a luminous dome
Of sapphire—seemed to float and sleep
Far in the front of its blue steep ;
And almost awful, none the less
For its liquescent loveliness,
Behind them sunk—just o'er the hill
The deep abyss, profound and still—
The so immediate Infinite ;
That yet emerged, the same, it seemed
In hue divine and melting balm,

In many a lake whose crystal calm
Uncrisped, unwrinkled, scarcely gleamed ;
Where sky above and lake below
Would like one sphere of azure show,
Save for the circling belt alone,
The softly-painted purple zone
Of mountains—bathed where nearer seen
In sunny tints of sober green,
With velvet dark of woods between,
All glossy glooms and shifting sheen ;
While here and there, some peak of snow
Would o'er their tenderer violet lean.

And yet within this region, fair
With wealth of waving woods—these glades
And glens and lustre-smitten shades,
Where trees of tropic beauty rare
With graceful spread and ample swell
Uprose—and that strange asphodel
On tufts of stiff green bayonet-blades,
Great bunches of white bloom upbore,
Like blocks of seawashed madrepore,
That steeped the noon in fragrance wide,
Till by the exceeding sweet opprest
The stately tree-fern leaned aside
For languor, with its starry crown
Of radiating fretted fans,
And proudly-springing beauteous crest
Of shoots all brown with glistening down,
Curved like the lyre-bird's tail half-spread,
Or necks opposed of wrangling swans,
Red bill to bill—black breast to breast,

Ay ! in this realm of seeming rest,
What sights you meet and sounds of dread !
Calcareous caldrons, deep and large
With geysers hissing to their marge ;
Sulphureous fumes that spout and blow ;
Columns and cones of boiling snow ;
And sable lazy-bubbling pools
Of sputtering mud that never cools ;
With jets of steam through narrow vents
Uproaring, maddening to the sky,
Like cannon-mouths that shoot on high
In unremitting loud discharge
Their inexhaustible contents ;
While oft beneath the trembling ground
Rumbles a drear persistent sound
Like ponderous engines infinite, working
At some tremendous task below !—
Such are the signs and symptoms—lurking
Or launching forth in dread display—
Of hidden fires, internal strife,
Amid that leafy, lush array
Of rank luxuriant verdurous life :
Glad haunts above where blissful love
Might revel, rove, enraptured dwell ;
But through them pierce such tokens fierce
Of rage beneath and frenzies fell ;
As if, to quench and stifle it,
Green Paradise were flung o'er Hell—
Flung fresh with all her bowers close-knit,
Her dewy vales and dimpled streams ;
Yet could not so its fury quell
But that the old red realm accurst
Would still recalcitrate, rebel,

Still struggle upward and outburst
In scalding fumes, sulphureous steams.
It struck you as you paused to trace
The sunny scenery's strange extremes,
As if in some divinest face,
All heavenly smiles, angelic grace,
Your eye at times discerned, despite
Sweet looks with innocence elate,
Some wan wild spasm of blank affright,
Or demon scowl of pent-up hate ;
Or some convulsive writhe confest,
For all that bloom of beauty bright,
An anguish not to be represt.
You look—a moment bask in, bless
Its laughing light of happiness ;
But look again—what startling throes
And fiery pangs of fierce distress
The lovely lineaments disclose—
How o'er the fascinating features flit
The genuine passions of the nether pit !

Alfred Domett.

XVI.

A Spring Afternoon in New Zealand.

WE rode in the shadowy place of pines,
  The wind went whispering here and there
  Like whispers in a house of prayer.
The sunshine stole in narrow lines,
  And sweet was the resinous atmosphere,
  The shrill cicada, far and near,
Piped on his high exultant third.

Summer ! Summer ! he seems to say—
Summer ! He knows no other word,
    But trills on it the live-long day ;
The little hawker of the green,
Who calls his wares through all the solemn forest scene.

A shadowy land of deep repose !
Here when the loud nor'wester blows,
How sweet, to soothe a trivial care,
The pine-trees' ever-murmured prayer !
To shake the scented powder down
    From stooping boughs that bar the way,
And see the vistas, golden brown,
    Touch the blue heaven far away.
But on and upward still we ride
    Whither the furze, an outlaw bold,
Scatters along the bare hillside
Handfuls of free, uncounted gold,
And breaths of nutty, wild perfume,
Salute us from the flowering broom.

I love this narrow, sandy road,
    That idly gads o'er hill and vale,
Twisting where once a rivulet flowed,
    With as many turns as a gossip's tale.
I love this shaky, creaking bridge,
And the willow leaning from the ridge,
    Shaped like some green fountain playing,
And the twinkling windows of the farm,
Just where the woodland throws an arm
    To hear what the merry stream is saying.

Stop the horses for a moment, high upon the breezy
    stair,
Looking over plain and upland, and the depth of
    summer air,
Watch the cloud and shadow sailing o'er the forest's
    sombre breast ;
Misty capes and snow-cliffs glimmer on the ranges to
    the west.
Hear the distant thunder rolling ; surely 'tis the making
    tide,
Swinging all the blue Pacific on the harbour's iron
    side....
Now the day grows grey and chill, but see on yonder
    wooded fold,
Between the clouds a ray of sunshine slips, and writes
    a word in gold.

                   Anne Glenny Wilson.

XVII.

The Pink and White Terraces.

FROM the low sky-line of the hilly range
  Before them, sweeping down its dark-green face
  Into the lake that slumbered at its base,
  A mighty Cataract—so it seemed—
  Over a hundred steps of marble streamed
  And gushed, or fell in dripping overflow—
  Flat steps, in flights half-circled—row o'er row,
  Irregularly mingling side by side ;
  They and the torrent-curtain wide,

All rosy-hued, it seemed, with sunset's glow.—
—But what is this !—no roar, no sound
Disturbs that torrent's hush profound !
The wanderers near and nearer come—
Still is the mighty Cataract dumb !
A thousand fairy lights may shimmer
With tender sheen, with glossy glimmer,
O'er curve advanced and salient edge
Of many a luminous water-ledge ;
A thousand slanting shadows pale
May fling their thin transparent veil
O'er deep recess and shadowy dent
In many a watery stair's descent :
Yet, mellow-bright, or mildly dim,
Both lights and shades—both dent and rim—
Each wavy streak, each warm snow-tress—
Stand rigid, mute and motionless !
No faintest murmur—not a sound—
Relieves that Cataract's hush profound ;
No tiniest bubble, not a flake
Of floating foam is seen to break
The smoothness where it meets the Lake :
Along that shining surface move
No ripples ; not the slightest swell
Rolls o'er the mirror darkly green,
Where, every feature limned so well—
Pale, silent and serene as death—
The cataract's image hangs beneath
The cataract—but not more serene,
More phantom-silent than is seen
The white rose-hued reality above.

They paddle past—for on the right
Another Cataract comes in sight ;
Another broader, grander flight
Of steps—all stainless, snowy-bright !
They land—their curious way they track
Near thickets made by contrast black ;
And then that wonder seems to be
A Cataract carved in Parian stone,
Or any purer substance known—
Agate or milk-chalcedony !
Its showering snow-cascades appear
Long ranges bright of stalactite,
And sparry frets and fringes white,
Thick-falling, plenteous, tier o'er tier ;
Its crowding stairs, in bold ascent
Piled up that silvery-glimmering height,
Are layers, they know—accretions slow
Of hard silicious sediment :
For as they gain a rugged road,
And cautious climb the solid rime,
Each step becomes a terrace broad—
Each terrace a wide basin brimmed
With water, brilliant, yet in hue
The tenderest, delicate harebell-blue
Deepening to violet !   Slowly climb
The twain, and turn from time to time
To mark the hundred baths in view—
Crystalline azure, snowy-rimmed—
The marge of every beauteous pond
Curve after curve—each lower beyond
The higher—outsweeping white and wide,
Like snowy lines of foam that glide

O'er level sea sands lightly skimmed
By thin sheets of the glistening tide.
   They climb those milk-white flats incrusted
And netted o'er with wavy ropes
Of wrinkled silica.   At last—
Each basin's heat increasing fast—
The topmost step the pair surmount,
And lo, the cause of all !   Around,
The circling cliffs a crater bound—
Cliffs damp with dark-green moss—their slopes
All crimson-stained with blots and streaks—
White-mottled and vermilion-rusted ;
And in the midst, beneath a cloud
That ever upward rolls and reeks
And hides the sky with its dim shroud,
Look where upshoots a fuming fount—
Up through a blue and boiling pool
Perennial—a great sapphire steaming,
In that coralline crater gleaming.
Upwelling ever, amethystal,
Ebullient comes the bubbling crystal !
Still growing cooler and more cool
As down the porcelain stairway slips
The fluid flint, and slowly drips,
And hangs each basin's curling lips
With crusted fringe each year increases,
Thicker than shear-forgotten fleeces ;
More close and regular than rows,
Long rows of snowy trumpet-flowers
Some day to hang in garden-bowers,
When strangers shall these wilds enclose.

But see ! in all that lively spread
Of blue and white and vermeil red,
How dark with growths of greenest gloss,
Just at the edge of that first ledge,
A little rocky islet peeps
Into the crater-caldron's deeps.
Along the ledge they lightly cross,
And from that place of vantage gaze
O'er all the scene—and every phase
The current takes as down it strays :
They note where'er, by step or stair,
By brimming bath, on hollow reef
Or hoary plain, its magic rain
Can reach a branch, a flower, a leaf—
The branching spray, leaf, blossom gay,
Are blanched and stiffened into stone !
So round about lurks tracery strewn
Of daintiest-moulded porcelain-ware,
Or coral wreaths and clusters rare,
A white flint-foliage ! rather say
Such fairy-work as frost alone
Were equal to, could it o'erlay
With tender crust of crystals fair,—
Fine spikes so delicately piled—
Not wintry trees, leafstripped and bare,
But summer's vegetation, rich and wild.

Alfred Domett.

XVIII.

Description of an Earthquake.

As through the land when some dread Earthquake
    thrills,
Shaking the hidden bases of the hills ;
Their grating adamantine depths, beneath
The ponderous, unimaginable strain and stress,
Groan shuddering as in pangs of worldwide death ;
While their long summits stretched against the sky
Rough-edged with trackless forests, to the eye
A double outline take (as when you press
The eyeball) ; and the beaten roads below
In yellow undulations roll and flow ;
And in broad swamps the serried flax-blades lithe,
Convulsed and tortured, rattling, toss and writhe,
As through them sweeps the swift tremendous throe :
Beasts howling run, or trembling, stand and stare,
And birds, as the huge tree-tops swing and rock,
Plunge scared into the more reliable air :—
All Nature wrung with spasm, affrighted reels
Aghast, as if the heavy chariot-wheels
Of God in very truth were thundering by
In too intolerable majesty :—
Then he who for the first time feels the shock,
Unconscious of its source, unguessing whence
Comes flying o'er him, with oppressive sense
Of irresistible Omnipotence,
That boundless, strange, o'erwhelming influence,
At once remote and in his inmost heart—
Is troubled most, that, with his staggering start

All the convictions from his birth upgrown,
And customary confidence, o'erthrown,
In Earth's eternal steadfastness, are gone.

Alfred Domett.

XIX.

To Pohutu in Ebullition.

WHENCE all this whiteness ?
This star-foam of brightness
  In fairy-like show ?
This marvellous spasm
Outleaping the chasm
  Of darkness below ?
Begotten in thunder,
The stormy depths under,
Thou awful white wonder—
Why travailest thou so ?

Below !   How infernal !
Above !   How supernal !
Effervescent—florescent
  White heat and white glow.
Erstwhile thou wert sleeping
And weirdly keeping
Thy mad pulse from leaping
  To vehement flow.

Oh, what are the powers
That force thy white showers
　　To such spectre-like play ?
Doth thy vicinity
Hold a divinity ?
　　Or otherwise ? say !

Is't a Titan in anguish ?
Doth Prometheus languish
　　In bowels of earth ?
Are Vulcans there ? forging
And hammering and scourging
　　To frustrate the birth
　　Of a spirit ?—infinite ?—
Escaping—uprising ;—
Now living—now dying,
Now flowing—now flying,
　　Retiring—expiring,
The exquisite vision
Sinks back to its prison.

　　　　　　　　　　Joyce Jocelyn.

XX.

Maoriland.

CHILD of Old Empire !　Best beloved, alone !
　The wizard moon and all her starry fays
　Have made their mirror in thy waterways,
Beneath the shadow of the red sun's throne :
When the sea-hero burst into thy zone
　Of Dreaming Silence, through the purple haze,
　What lucid visions lit his raptured gaze,
What heart-hopes sang to ocean's monotone !

And he, perchance, hath joy of thee to-day,
  Who won thee from the unrelenting gale,
    The hopeless calm and the inconstant breeze ;
Where, out beyond Death's sea-track, worlds away,
  The winds are wooed by his triumphant sail
    To mad airs and sonorous symphonies.

D. M. Ross.

XXI.

A New Zealand Picture.

OTAKI, that rollest in thy pride,
  First among the rivers far and near,
  Little streamlet, flowing blue and clear,
Ocean, with your strong imperious tide.

Russet bushes, sandhills waste and wide,
  Pointed flax blades, shining vivid green,
  Scarlet spotted spiders, rarely seen
Save by those who know where you abide.

Grey and orange grass, that creeps to bind
  Shifting sands and bid them stay and rest,
Dear and lovely are you all in kind.

Each is touched with a peculiar grace ;
  And the soul that loves and watches, best
Learns the wonders of this happy place.

Mary E. Richmond.

XXII.

Tauranga.

CURVING and wandering by a wandering shore
  Of endless sunny beaches moves the sea,
  Spilling its wealth of shell and weed, while we
Watch peacefully, or dip a silent oar.

And as the evening gathers more and more
  That strange old Mount purples mysteriously,
  And Waharoa and Haramiki
Creep down to watch the places of their War,

Tuhua, Motiti and Karewha,
  And the sad stretch of Matakana sand,
  Like some great monster in his idle ease !
Frowns still from Maunganui the desert Pa,
But all the beaches sleep and all the land,
  And only sea-birds now disturb the seas.

Erica R. Wilson.

XXIII.

Stewart Island.

THERE are great seas that flutter to the coast
  As some giant sea-bird spent ;
There's a green bushland that has no other boast
  Than that it clothes content.

And all about the islets studded are,
  They laugh back to the sea,
While out beyond the big ships battle far
  Into immensity.

S. G. August.

XXIV.

Wednesday.

COME, let's be friends—this day of bliss
　　Was surely meant for happy eyes—
Or sign, at least, an armistice
　　Till quarrelling winds arise.

On this green headland we will stay
　　Till day has spent his golden hoard ;
See the cloud-shadows on the Bay
　　Mark out a chequer-board.

These ships shall be our playing men ;
　　Mine is the schooner, calm-bestead ;
Yours is the brig that tacks in vain
　　To clear the Burning Head.

Mine, mine has won !　She fills, she soars,
　　She sails into the azure day ;
A wild wind shakes the mountain doors,
　　And sweeps our board away !

Anne Glenny Wilson.

XXV.

Fairyland.

Do you remember that careless band,
Riding o'er meadow and wet sea-sand,
　　One autumn day, in a mist of sunshine,
Joyously seeking for fairyland ?

The wind in the tree-tops was scarcely heard,
The streamlet repeated its one silver word,
    And far away, o'er the depths of woodland,
Floated the bell of the parson-bird.

Pale hoar-frost glittered in shady slips,
Where ferns were dipping their finger-tips,
    From mossy branches a faint perfume
Breathed over honeyed clematis lips.

At last we climbed to the ridge on high :
Ah, crystal vision !   Dreamland nigh !
    Far, far below us, the wide Pacific
Slumbered in azure from sky to sky.

And cloud and shadow, across the deep
Wavered, or paused in enchanted sleep,
    And eastward, the purple-misted islets
Fretted the wave with terrace and steep.

We looked on the tranquil, glassy bay,
On headlands sheeted with dazzling spray,
    And the whitening ribs of a wreck forlorn
That for twenty years had wasted away.

All was so calm, and pure and fair,
It seemed the hour of worship there,
    Silent, as where the great North Minster
Rises for ever, a visible prayer.

Then we turned from the murmurous forest-land,
And rode over shingle and silver sand,
    For so fair was the earth in the golden autumn,
We sought no farther for Fairyland.

Anne Glenny Wilson.

XXVI.

The Forty-Mile Bush.

FAR through the forest's aromatic glade
  We rode one afternoon of golden ease.
The long road ran through sunshine and through shade,
  Lulled by the somnolent stories of the trees.

Sometimes a bell-bird fluted far away ;
  Sometimes the murmur of the leafy deep,
Rising and falling through the autumnal day,
  Sang louder on the hills, then sank to sleep.

Before us stretched the pine-trees' sombre miles,
  Soft lay the moss, like furs upon the floor ;
Behind, the woodland's green monotonous aisles,
  Closed far away by sunset's amber door.

League after league the same.   The sky grew red,
  And through the trees appeared a snowy gleam
Of lonely peak and spectral mountain-head,
  And gulfs that nurse the glacier and the stream.

Deep in the glen, the merry waters racing
  Sent forth their turbulent voices to the night ;
The stars above began their solemn pacing,
  And home-like shone the distant village light.

Mysterious forest !   In this humming city
  I seem to hear thy music-breathing tree,
Thy branches wave and beckon me in pity,
  To seek again thy hospitality !

Anne Glenny Wilson.

XXVII.

The Passing of the Forest.

A Lament for the Children of Tané.

All glory cannot vanish from the hills.
   Their strength remains, their stature of command
O'er shadowy valleys that cool twilight fills
   For wanderers weary in a faded land ;
Refreshed when rain-clouds swell a thousand rills,
   Ancient of days in green old age they stand,
Though lost the beauty that became Man's prey
When from their flanks he stripped the woods away.

But thin their vesture now—the trembling grass
   Shivering and yielding as the breeze goes by,
Catching quick gleams and scudding shades that pass
   As running seas reflect a windy sky.
A kinglier garb their forest raiment was
   From crown to feet that clothed them royally,
Shielding the secrets of their streams from day
Ere the deep, sheltering woods were hewn away.

Well may these brooding, mutilated kings,
   Stripped of the robes that ages weaved, discrowned,
Draw down the clouds with soft-enfolding wings
   And white, aerial fleece to wrap them round,
To hide the scars that every season brings,
   The fire's black smirch, the landslip's gaping wound,
Well may they shroud their heads in mantle grey
Since from their brows the leaves were plucked away !

Gone is the forest's labyrinth of life,
    Its clambering, thrusting, clasping, throttling race,
Creeper with creeper, bush with bush at strife,
    Struggling in silence for a breathing space ;
Below, a realm with tangled rankness rife,
    Aloft, tree columns in victorious grace.
Gone the dumb hosts in warfare dim ; none stay ;
Dense brake and stately trunk have passed away.

Gone are those gentle forest-haunting things,
    Eaters of honey, honey-sweet in song.
The tui and the bell-bird—he who rings
    That brief, rich music we would fain prolong,
Gone the woodpigeon's sudden whirr of wings,
    The daring robin all unused to wrong,
Ay, all the friendly friendless creatures.   They
Lived with their trees and died and passed away.

Gone are the flowers.   The kowhai like ripe corn,
    The frail convolvulus, a day-dream white,
And dim-hued passion-flowers for shadows born,
    Wan orchids strange as ghosts of tropic night ;
The blood-red rata strangling trees forlorn
    Or with exultant scarlet fiery bright
Painting the sombre gorges, and that fay
The starry clematis are all away !

Lost is the resinous, sharp scent of pines,
    Of wood fresh cut, clean-smelling for the hearth,
Of smoke from burning logs in wavering lines
    Softening the air with blue, of brown, damp earth
And dead trunks fallen among coiling vines,
    Slow-mouldering, moss-coated.   Round the girth
Of the green land the wind brought vale and bay
Fragrance far-borne now faded all away.

Lost is the sense of noiseless sweet escape
    From dust of stony plain, from sun and gale,
When the feet tread where quiet shadows drape
    Dark stems with peace beneath a kindly veil.
No more the pleasant rustlings stir each shape,
    Creeping with whisperings that rise and fail
Through glimmering lace-work lit by chequered play
Of light that danced on moss now burned away.

Gone are the forest tracks where oft we rode
    Under the silvery fern fronds, climbing slow
Through long green tunnels, while hot noontide glowed
    And glittered on the tree-tops far below.
There in the stillness of the mountain road
    We just could hear the valley river flow
With dreamy murmur through the slumbering day
Lulling the dark-browed woods now passed away.

Fanned by the dry, faint air that lightly blew
    We watched the shining gulfs in noonday sleep
Quivering between tall cliffs that taller grew
    Above the unseen torrent calling deep,
Till like a sword cleaving the foliage through
    The waterfall flashed foaming down the steep,
White, living water, cooling with its spray
Fresh plumes of curling fern now scorched away.

The axe bites deep.   The rushing fire streams bright ;
    Swift, beautiful and fierce it speeds for Man,
Nature's rough-handed foeman, keen to smite
    And mar the loveliness of ages.   Scan
The blackened forest ruined in a night,
    The sylvan Parthenon that God will plan
But builds not twice.   Ah, bitter price to pay
For Man's dominion—beauty swept away !

                            William Pember Reeves.

XXVIII.

Dead Timber.

THESE are not ours—the isles of columned whiteness,
　　Set in an old and legend-whispering sea ;
Nor crowning domes that take the morning's brightness,
　　Praising the Lord in open majesty ;
Nor arches' hushed eternal invocation ;
　　Nor windows glowing with the love of God ;
Nor slender minarets that take their station,
　　Like spears ascending where the faithful trod.

There, on the hillside, is our nation's building,
　　The tall dead trees so bare against the sky.
They neither kiss the morn nor take the sunset's gliding ;
　　They hear no brimming prayer, no sinner's cry.
But in the desolation of our making,
　　Where prey at will the sun and wind and rain,
They call the sky to witness of our breaking,
　　They tell the stars the story of our gain.

Unranked and formless, stark they stand, unheeding
　　The whisper of their brothers soon to die.
Their hearts are dry from the bright axe's bleeding,
　　And dead the music of their leaves' long sigh.
Mute in their misery of devastation,
　　They hold between us and the living light,
In twisted agony of revelation,
　　The lifeless litter of the field of fight.

Yet if some ask : " Where is your art, your writing
　　By which we know that you have aught to say ? "
We shall reply : " Yonder, the hill-crest blighting,
　　There is our architecture's blazoned way.

This monument we fashioned in our winning,
   A gibbet for the beauty we have slain ;
Behold the flower of our art's beginning,
   The jewel in the circlet of her reign ! "

Yet, so doth patient beauty work, subduing
   The very husks of death to gracious ends ;
The heavy plodding days, their task pursuing,
   Slowly transmute these victims into friends.
Dwelling with them, we take them to our living,
   Looking on them, we wed them to our sight.
Resting with us, they grant us their forgiving,
   And creep into the round of our delight.

Less were the dawn in miracle unfolding,
   Did these return not to the breathless hill.
Disturbed the heart, known loveliness beholding,
   Did these not watch us as the hours fill.
Strange were the hush of eve by mists enchanted,
   Did these not stand to catch the floating flowers,
Common the moonlight by the shadows haunted
   But for the mystery of these lightless towers.

Some day our feet may walk where art is golden ;
   Then round our hearts will lap the tides of time.
We shall be one with dwellings rich and olden,
   And fragrant prospects sweet with ancient rhyme.
Yet, though we go where memories come thronging,
   And wonder leads us wheresoe'er we roam,
Through our delight will creep the voice of longing—
   O dear dead timber on the hills of home !

                                        Alan E. Mulgan.

XXIX.

The Last of the Forest.

HAST thou not heard, O White Man, through a troubled
    dreaming
  On some still night when all the world lay stark,
Sharp through the silence, moaning of the sea, and
    screaming
             Of night-birds in the dark ?

Hast thou not said, O White Man, shivering when the
    shrieking
  Wild voices thrilled thee in a mystery of pain :
" Peace ! 'tis the Ocean calling ! 'tis the Dead Tree
    creaking !
             Hush thee, my heart, again ! "

Are they but birds ? is it the sea in lamentation,
  Or is it Ghosts of Earth, and Air, that cry,
Moaning a requiem, in their utter desolation,
             For old worlds passing by ?

Is it the wind that howls? The Dead Tree thou ignorest,
  Speech hath, and Spirit, though a shadow grey.
Hearest thou not the voice that mourns the vanished
    Forest,
             That was, and passed away ?

" White Man, behold me ! ghastly in the Spring's
    sereneness,
  Battered, and bruised, by ceaseless storm and strife ;
I am the Spectre of a mighty forest's greenness,
            I, who am Death in Life !

Late, and with lingering footsteps, Spring draws near,
        revealing
    Love, and new life, to every passer-by ;
Angel belovëd ! in thy touches is no healing,
            No balm for such as I !

Dawn after dawn, I, sleepless, wait the first faint flushes,
    Then, as the cloud-gates of the East unfold,
Over the world the red flood of the sunrise rushes
            That leaves me white and cold.

Heaven in her pity rains her tender tears upon me,
    Me,—who shall never bud nor bloom again,
There is no quickening in the sunshine lavished on me,
            The dew drops all in vain.

Shattered by lightning, tempest-tossed, and torn, and
        broken,
    Storms had no power to shake me till this last,
When, at the coming of the White Man, doom was
        spoken,—
            Now live I in the Past !

What is there left, O White Man, what is there remain-
        ing ?
    What is there flees not from before thy face ?
Wonder thou not to hear the Spirits' loud complaining
            For flower, forest, race !

As the worn body by a lingering breath is haunted,
    So is my Ghost withheld from final peace ;
While these strong roots thus firmly in the earth are
        planted,
            Am I denied release.

Hast thou no mercy, Storm-wind ? let thy fury hound
    me ;
  Let loose thy Fiends, and bid them work their will,
Till in Earth's bosom snaps the link that bound me !
        Then shall my soul be still ! "

Dost thou not hear, O White Man, through thy troubled
    dreaming
  On this calm night when all the world lies stark,
Sharp through the silence, moaning of the sea, and
    screaming
        Of night-birds in the dark ?

What ! dost thou say, O White Man, shivering when
    the shrieking
  Wild voices thrill thee in an agony of pain :
" Peace ! 'tis the Ocean calling ! 'tis the Dead Tree
    creaking !
        Hush thee, my heart, again ! "

They are not birds ! the sea wails not in lamentation—
  They are the Ghosts of Earth, of Air, that cry,
Moaning a requiem, in their utter desolation,
        For old worlds passing by.

                        Dora Wilcox.

XXX.

The Old Botanist's Farewell to the Southern Alps.

FAREWELL to the moorlands, farewell to the mountains,
    Farewell to the dark cliff and deep-shadowed dingle !
No more shall I drink from the icy cold fountains
    That gush in their glory from out the grey shingle.

No more shall I watch from the high windy ridges
    The cloud-shadows drifting with indolent motion,
The bright silver rivers, the gossamer bridges,
    The far margin lit with the gleam of the ocean.

No more shall I snatch in the high holy places,
    Where the Maker of Mountains is marvellously
        shrouded,
The glance brief and swift upon infinite spaces,
    The surge in the soul and the vision unclouded.

No more shall I climb in the pale dawn with passion,
    The dew from the snowgrass with eager feet shaking,
And hear the nor'-west wind come charging and crashing
    And break on the sharp rocks with tumult and
        quaking.

No more shall I see on a day of still weather
    Far range upon range to infinity dwindle,
Snow-crowned and ice-girdled, all slumbering together,
    Erebus and Arrowsmith and d'Archiac and Tyndall.

No more shall you charm me, dear dainty Ourisia,
    You broad fields of mountain-musk starred with
      white blossom,
Euphrasia, Raoulia, Phyllachne, Celmisia,
    No more shall you strike the deep chord in my bosom.

No more shall I pore on the hard tawny grasses
    That colour the steep spurs and long level reaches,
No more shall I haunt the high desolate passes
    Where the elfinwood sprawls on the fringe of the
      beeches.

No more shall I see, as the high sun is westering,
    In the steep dusky valleys that look to his setting,
Thin streams in the late light all twining and glistering,
    Like threads of fine silver the purple gloom fretting.

No more shall I hear the white mountain gull crying
    Among the bare rocks where the great gusts go
      booming,
Six thousand feet up where in rough hollows lying,
    The broody old tarns hang a-drowsing and glooming.

I shall see them far off in the magical distance,
    With bloom like a ripe plum, so fresh and so tender,
They will beckon and woo me and call with insistence,
    The big shining Alps in their pomp and their splen-
      dour.

But I camp no more in the beech-wooded valleys,
    No more shall I sleep in the roar of the river
Or wander alone in the cool shady alleys,
    For my feet have come down to the lowlands for ever.

                    Arnold Wall.

XXXI.

Ver Sacrum.

SOFT is the sun, and soft is the air, and soft is the
 Mother's breast ;
Soft is the song she crooneth as I stretch me there to
 rest—
Song with its warp of wooing wind, and its weft of
 birdnotes clear :
How the heart it stills, and thrills, and fills. . . .
'Tis Spring—oh, Spring is here !

David Will. M. Burn.

XXXII.

A Song of Winter.

BIRD on the leafless bough,
 Summer has fled ;
Bird on the leafless bough,
 Flowers are dead.

Dead too thy trilling song,
 Dead in thy grief ;
Not e'en a saddened song
 Mourns for the leaf.

E'en now on leafless bough
 Swells the small bud,
Soon all the leafy bough
 Blossoms shall stud.

Then 'mid the summer leaves,
  Winter forgot,
Singing 'mid summer leaves,
  Thy happy lot.

Why then, poor stricken soul,
  Why dost thou grieve ?
Thou knowest, stricken soul,
  Time will relieve.

Ah ! will not mem'ry keep
  Sharp grief alive ?
Never will mem'ry sleep
  Howe'er I strive.

Alexander Bathgate.

XXXIII.

A Winter Daybreak.

I.

FROM the dark gorge, where burns the morning star,
  I hear the glacier river rattling on
And sweeping o'er his ice-ploughed shingle-bar,
  While wood-owls shout in sombre unison,
And fluttering southern dancers glide and go ;
And black swan's airy trumpets wildly, sweetly blow.

II.

The cock crows in the windy winter morn,
  Then must I rise and fling the curtain by.
  All dark ! But for a strip of fiery sky
Behind the ragged mountains, peaked and torn.

One planet glitters in the icy cold,
Poised like a hawk above the frozen peaks ;
   And bends the cypress, shuddering, to his fold,
While every timber, every casement creaks.
   But still the skylarks sing aloud and bold ;
The wooded hills arise ; the white cascade
Shakes with wild laughter all the silent shadowy glade.

III.

Now from the shuttered East a silvery bar
Shines through the mist, and shows the mild day-star.
The storm-wrapped peaks start out and fade again,
And rosy vapours skirt the pastoral plain ;
The garden paths with hoary rime are wet ;
And sweetly breathes the winter violet ;
The jonquil half unfolds her ivory cup,
With clouds of gold-eyed daisies waking up.

IV.

Pleasant it is to turn and see the fire
Dance on the hearth, as he would never tire ;
The home-baked loaf, the Indian bean's perfume,
Fill with their homely cheer the panelled room.
Come, crazy storm ! and thou, wild glittering hail,
Rave o'er the roof and wave your icy veil ;
Shout in our ears, and take your madcap way !
I laugh at storms ! for Roderick comes to-day.

Anne Glenny Wilson.

XXXIV.

Morning.

Morning passes, never ceases,
Day-break laughs on earth for ever.

Now is the hour of the morning's prime,—
　List to the voices ;—sea-sprites hymning !
Wispy clouds from the sea-haze climb,
　Rosy gulls in the gold sea swimming :
　　Waves defying Time's ageing hand
　　Dance to the gleaming sand.

Now is the hour of the morning's prime,—
　Earth lies laughing and Heaven bends **over :**
Bees are a-hum in the banks of thyme,
　Bees are a-drone in the fields of clover :
　　Poppies and cornflowers gem the corn,
　　And a new world smiles, dew-born.

Now is the hour of the morning's prime,—
　Ho,—the revel of rival thrushes !
That's a blackbird hid in the lime,
　Clearly the lark's lay fills the hushes :
　　Silver hazes and cloud-wefts sever,—
　　And such morns break for ever.

Johannes C. Andersen.

XXXV.

A Night in Spring.

THE high, white, windy stars
  Their naked beams flash through
The boughs of budding orchard trees.
  The wind has dried the dew,

And with its wide soft sweep
  Makes sounds along the grass,
As if one with a trailing gown
  Deliberately did pass.

No summer sweetness yet,
  No showers of lavish bloom,
But from the swelling bark and buds
  A ghostly faint perfume.

It is the season's youth,
  Austerely pure and fair ;
A hint of splendours yet to be
  Comes with the wandering air.

The soul of my young love
  Is like this clear spring night,
As high and starry as the skies,
  As coldly sweet and bright.

Ah ! would she walked with me,
  In the windy stir of air,
The sweet grass underneath her feet,
  And stars caught in her hair.

Our hands would clasp and cling,
   As 'neath the boughs we passed,
And the love that almost breaks my heart
   Would waken hers at last.

               Alice A. Kenny.

XXXVI.

" Good-night."

" To each and all a fair ' Good-night.' "—Scott.

    " GOOD-NIGHT : "
So, hand firm clasping hand,
   We meetly close the day,
Unconscious that the angel band
   Bend down to hear us say
      " Good-night."
In tender tones, or grave, or light ;
For in their paradise all bright
They never, never say " Good-night."

    " Good-night : "
From cot and curtained bed
   The sweet child-accents come,
Tired sprites who love to tread
   Where daisies grow and brown bees hum—
      " Good-night."
In rosy dreams each past delight
Again will bless their happy sight,
So drowsily they lisp, " Good-night."

" Good-night,"
The silver stars proclaim
In their own grand, soft speech,
While woodland warblers frame
And utter in the twilight, each,
" Good-night."
With sudden, daring, darting flight
From blackthorn hedge to cedar height,
They twitter, chirp, or trill, " Good-night."

M. A. Sinclair.

XXXVII.

Nightfall.

SWEEP up, oh ! wind of night, from out the eastward,
Sweep down, oh ! mist of night, as dies the day ;
Sweep low between us and the mountain ranges,
And hide the stars away.

Hide all the hope of day, oh ! night of shadows ;
The moon's bright promise, and the noontide's light.
Take all the outside world for your possession—
Oh ! phantoms of the night.

Within are lights you cannot hide or darken,
Spirits of nightfall, wheresoe'er you roam ;
The light of fires upon the home-hearth burning,
Heart-love within the home.

Mary H. Poynter.

XXXVIII.

The Dying of the Day.

UPON a couch with gorgeous splendours drest
Day lay a-dying in the amber West,
Silent and sad, for since his race begun
He had known much of sorrow 'neath the sun ;

Bereft of all his children, the fair Hours,
That bloomed and faded like the summer flowers,
Save one, the last, of all-surpassing charms
That lay a-dying with him, in his arms :

And sorrowful the royal couch beside
Sat pale-browed Evening, the old monarch's bride,
Lovely in grief as tearfully she smiled
Upon her hoary spouse and sunny child.

Silence reigned all around, for Nature's choir
Had hushed their songs to view the god expire ;
And she stood tip-toe, and with bated breath
Watched through the casement the old monarch's death.

And soon it came ; the lifelight left his eye,
And through the palace windows came a sigh,
Deep-drawn and faint, from out the distant West
As of one weary sinking into rest ;

The Hour was gone, and with it died the Day,
And o'er them Evening threw a pall of grey,
Then kissed the placid features of the dead,
And drew her dusky curtains round the bed ;

Then lighting up a star she hung it high,
For a pale corpse-light, in the fading sky,
And as from out their lairs began to creep
The sombre shadows she went forth to weep ;

And up and down the garden Earth she passed,
And as she walked her tears fell thick and fast ;
And then returning with a solemn tread,
She robed herself in mourning for the dead,
And clothed in black, but crowned with jewels bright,
Went forth to watch until the morning light.

William Jukes Steward.

XXXIX.

After Sunset.

OVER my head the skylark singeth,
  Though the sun hath set and the night draws nigh ;
What is the message the sweet song bringeth ?
  Is it a hint that a day gone by—
Gone by—gone by—may return again,
And the time of waiting go past like rain ?

The lark still sings as he upward flieth
  Through the dusk-blue air, and the notes drop down
To the listening earth, and my heart that crieth
  For the breath of spring and the summer's crown.
Ah ! crown of summer, dost hang as far
As over the skylark that lone white star ?

Oh, lonely star !   But the song hath ended,
  The purple mountains grow darker yet ;
Soon will the crimson and grey be blended,
  And nought to tell where the sun hath set ;
The blue dusk deepens, more stars there be :
What is the promise ye hold for me ?

Where the hills drop down to the sea which spurneth,
  For ever and ever, the patient land ;
Where the blue hills melt to the blue sky, burneth
  A distant fire like a love-lit brand.
My path descends, and it goes from sight,
But I know it is strong for the coming night.

O stars and fire ! is your inward meaning
  To tell of a day which is yet to be ?
Of an hour when Time shall go backward leaning
  To pluck white roses and red for me ?
When the joy which is past shall come back—come
    back—
With a threefold strength that shall nothing lack ?

Clara Singer Poynter.

XL.

In the Moonlight.

THE moon is bright, and the winds are laid, and the
    river is roaring by ;
Orion swings, with his belted lights low down in the
    western sky ;
North and south from the mountain gorge to the heart
    of the silver plain

There's many an eye will see no sleep till the east grows
    bright again ;
There's many a hand will toil to-night, from the centre
    down to the sea ;
And I'm far from the men I used to know—and my love
    is far from me.

Where the broad flood eddies the dredge is moored to
    the beach of shingle white,
And the straining cable whips the stream in a spray of
    silver light ;
The groaning buckets bear their load, and the engine
    throbs away,
And the wash pours red on the turning screen that
    knows not night or day ;
For there's many an ounce of gold to save, from the
    gorge to the shining sea—
And there's many a league of the bare brown hills
    between my love and me.

Where the lines of gorse are parched and dry, and the
    sheaves are small and thin,
The engine beats and the combine sings to the drays
    that are leading in,
For they're thrashing out of the stook to-night, and
    the plain is as bright as day,
And the fork-tines flash as the sheaves are turned on
    the frame of the one-horse dray ;
For many a hand will toil to-night, from the mountains
    down to the sea ;—
But I'm far from the lips of the girl I love, and the
    heart that beats for me.

The trappers are out on the hills to-night, and the
    sickly lantern-shine
Is mocking the gleam of the silver moon in the scrub on
    the long trap-line ;
The tallies are big on the rock-strewn spur, and the
    rattling clink of the chain
Comes weirdly mixed from the moon-bright hill with
    the whistling shriek of pain ;
For many a hand will toil to-night where the tussocks
    are waving free ;—
But it's over the hills and over the plain to the heart
    that beats for me.

The stars are bright, and the night is still, and the
    river is singing by,
And many a face is upward turned to gaze at the moon's
    bright eye.
North and south, from the forest deeps to the heart of
    the silver plain,
There's many an eye will see no sleep till the east grows
    bright again ;
There's many a hand will toil to-night by shining land
    and sea.
O moonlight, bear my message of love to the heart that
    beats for me.

David McKee Wright.

XLI.

Spring Fires.

THE running rings of fire on the Canterbury hills,
 Running, ringing, dying at the border of the snow !
Mad, young, seeking, as a young thing wills,
 The ever, ever-living, ever-buried Long Ago !

The soft running fire on the Canterbury hills,
 Swinging low the censer of a tender heathenesse
To the dim Earth goddesses that quicken all the thrills,
 When the heart's wine of August is dripping from
  the press !

The quiet bloom of haze on the Canterbury hills !
 The fire, it is the moth that is winging to the snow,
Oh, pure red moth, but the sweet white kills :
 And we thrill again to watch you, but we know, but
  we know !

The long yellow spurs on the Canterbury hills
 To a moon of maiden promise waken once in all the
  year,
When the fires come again and the little tui trills,
 And who will name or think on a January sere ?

The lone, large flower of the Canterbury hills
  On the slender ti-tree will hang her honeyed head
When the moon of fire has called her to the spurs and
    the rills,
  Dim and strong and typical of tintless river-bed.

The scent of burning tussock on the Canterbury hills,
  The richness and the mystery that waken like a lyre
With the dearness of a dreaming that never yet fulfils !—
  And we know it, and we know it, but we love the
    moon of fire !

                              Jessie Mackay.

XLII.

In Town.

WE came from the hills where the hot winds blow
  And the yellow tussocks wave,
From the long, bright plain where the titris grow,
From the land of the sun, and the frost, and snow,
  Where the hearts are strong and brave.

We had kept the lines in the winter-time
  On the wing of the poisoning gang.
From rock to rock in the mountain climb,
When the frosts were keen and the air like wine,
  And the shingle faces rang.

When the speargrass fire was burning bright,
  We had sat in the magic ring—
When the knives were swift and the hearts were light,
With a thousand skins to clean at night,
  And one had a song to sing.

We're in town, and we met in the noisy street,
  And the old strong days came back—
The wind in the tussocks waving sweet,
The mountain ridge, and the plain at our feet,
  And the winding rocky track.

The bustling town, with its pink and green,
  And its hoardings of red and blue,
To our open eyes was poor and mean
As we thought of the long, bright days that had been
  In the old fair world we knew.

The church spires climb to the dreary sky,
  And the bells ring peace from Heaven ;
But the joy of God's rich fields that lie
Wide to the winds and the wild bird's cry
  May never again be given.

Yet here in the clasp of a friendly hand
  That wrought with me side by side,
I feel the thrill of the mountain land,
The life of toil that was strong and grand,
  Old Memory's rich flood-tide.

David McKee Wright.

XLIII.

Arlington.

THE sun shines bright on Arlington, the drowsy sheep
    creep by,
The water races seam the hills, cloud shadows line the
    sky,
New fences climb the warm brown spurs to guard the
    scrubber ewes,
Because the run is broken up for hungry cockatoos ;
The township sleeps below the hill, the homestead on
    the plain,
But the lost days of Arlington will never come again.

The working-men are seen no more in hut or rabbit
    camp,
The stock-whip never will be heard about the river
    swamp ;
No more the mighty fleeces crown the bins like drifted
    snow,
No more the princely rams go down, the wonder of the
    show ;
The swagger on the weary tramp comes o'er the sum-
    mer plain,
And sighs for rest at Arlington, yet knows he sighs in
    vain.

There's little work on Arlington since the old station
    days ;
The hawk-faced owners groan to tell sheep-farming
    never pays,
They build no homesteads on the runs, they pay no
    wages out ;
The station style was different when money flew about.
The rabbits flourish on the hills and burrow all the plain,
The stock that ran on Arlington will never run again.

The good old boss of Arlington was everybody's friend,
He liked to keep the wages up right to the very end ;
If diggers' horses went astray they always could be
    found,
The cow that roamed across the run was never in the
    pound.
He was a white man through and through, cheery and
    fair and plain,
And now he'll never ride the rounds of Arlington again.

David McKee Wright.

XLIV.

The Old Place.

So the last day's come at last, the close of my fifteen
    year—
The end of the hope, an' the struggles, an' messes
    I've put in here.
All of the shearing's over, the final mustering done,—
Eleven hundred and fifty for the incoming man, near on.
Over five thousand I drove 'em, mob by mob, down
    the coast ;
Eleven-fifty in fifteen year....it isn't much of a boast.

Oh, it's a bad old place ! Blown out o' your bed half
    the nights,
And in summer the grass burnt shiny an' bare as your
    hand, on the heights :
The creek dried up by November, and in May a thunder-
    ing roar

That carries down toll o' your stock to salt 'em whole
    on the shore.
Clear'd I have, and I've clear'd an' clear'd, yet every-
    where, slap in your face,
Briar, tauhinu, an' ruin !   God ! it's a brute of a place.
....An' the house got burnt which I built, myself,
    with all that worry and pride ;
Where the Missus was always homesick, and where she
    took fever, and died.

Yes, well ! I'm leaving the place.   Apples look red
    on that bough.
I set the slips with my own hand.   Well—they're the
    other man's now.
The breezy bluff : an' the clover that smells so over
    the land,
Drowning the reek of the rubbish, that plucks the profit
    out o' your hand :
That bit o' Bush paddock I fall'd myself, an' watched,
    each year, come clean
(Don't it look fresh in the tawny ?   A scrap of Old-
    Country green) :
This air, all healthy with sun an' salt, an' bright with
    purity :
An' the glossy karakas there, twinkling to the big blue
    twinkling sea :
Ay, the broad blue sea beyond, an' the gem-clear cove
    below,
Where the boat I'll never handle again, sits rocking to
    and fro :
There's the last look to it all ! an' now for the last upon

This room, where Hetty was born, an' my Mary died,
    an' John

Well, I'm leaving the poor old place, and it cuts as keen
    as a knife ;

The place that's broken my heart—the place where I've
    lived my life.

B. E. Baughan.

XLV.

The Whare.

IT stands upon the grassy slope,
    A ruin, brown and lone :
The door swings on its hinge of rope
    With strange and dismal tone,
Whene'er the wandering winds that pass
Bear with them, o'er the thistled grass,
    The darksome forest's moan.

Lone seems it when on all around
    The summer moon lies still ;
When not a zephyr stirs to sound
    The rata on the hill :
When but the locust on the tree
Adds to the murmur of the bee
    Its tuneless note and shrill.

Here, mouldering walls stand rent and dark,
    Once wind-and-weather proof ;
There, strips of brown manuka-bark
    Drop from the tattered roof ;
And wandering cattle, wild as wind,
Upon the sward have left behind
    The print of many a hoof.

No more, when with its burden black
   Low broods the winter night,
Shall shine through every chimney crack
   The back-log's yellow light.
The bushman's tiring task is done ;
And stumps, that rot in rain and sun,
   Stand bleached to spectral white.

Lone whare, on the green hill-side,
   From human haunts apart,
Unnoticed by the eye of Pride,
   A hallowed spot thou art.
This roof, that ever inward falls,
This shattered door, these mouldering walls,
   Once held a human heart.
              H. L. Twisleton.

XLVI.

The Bush Mother.

THE Kowhai swings above me
   A crown of glittering gold,
And all along the valley
   New life and love unfold.
The world is fair and fragrant,
   And hither, with the Spring,
Back to the old Bush-Mother
   One comes a-wandering !

The shy Bush-children gather,
   And peer from every bough :
" And who is it comes hither,
   Lost Brother, is it thou ?

Strange, strange art thou, O Brother,
    Hast been so long away
That neither word, nor whisper,
    Has power to charm to-day ! "

What turmoil lies behind me !
    The city, and the street,
The struggle, and the discord,
    The clang of hurrying feet,—
O Mother, tender Mother,
    Back to thy peace I come,
O put thine arms around me,
    Thy Prodigal, who's Home !

Thou wast my Nurse and Teacher,
    And I, thy foster child,
Am kin to all thy nurslings
    So fresh, and free, and wild :
Thy Birds, they were my Brothers,
    Thy Streams, my Sisters dear
Who taught me many a ballad
    That only Bushfolk hear.

Thine elder sons and daughters
    Told many tales to me ;—
Thy Rata, clad in crimson,
    So wonderful to see !
Thy Kowhai, Thy Konini,
    Thy Totara so tall,—
Hid in thy wildernesses
    I knew and loved them all !

O Mother, tender Mother,
   Thy spell is on me yet ;
Thy spirit on my spirit,
   Thy peace upon my fret.
Put thou thine arms around me,
   I nestle to thy breast ;
Thou hast for mourners comfort,
   And for the toilers rest.

O we who dwell in cities
   May journey far from thee ;
But still we hear thee calling,
   Calling o'er land and sea ;
And when the world is radiant
   And fragrant with the Spring,
Back to the old Bush-Mother
   Her babes come wandering !

Dora Wilcox.

XLVII.

While the Billy Boils.

THE speargrass crackles under the billy and overhead
   is the winter sun ;
There's snow on the hills, there's frost in the gully,
   that minds me of things that I've seen and done,
Of blokes that I knew, and mates that I've worked
   with, and the sprees we had in the days gone by ;
And a mist comes up from my heart to my eyelids, I
   feel fair sick and I wonder why.

There is coves and coves! Some I liked partic'lar,
    and some I would sooner I never knowed;
But a bloke can't choose the chaps that he's thrown
    with in the harvest paddock or here on the road.
There was chaps from the other side that I shore with
    that I'd like to have taken along for mates,
But we said, " So long! " and we laughed and parted
    for good and all at the station gates.

I mind the time when the snow was drifting and Billy
    and me was out for the night—
We lay in the lee of a rock, and waited, hungry and
    cold, for the morning light.
Then he went one way and I the other—we'd been like
    brothers for half a year;
He said: " I'll see you again in town, mate, and we'll
    blow the froth off a pint of beer."

He went to a job on the plain he knowed of and I went
    poisoning out at the back,
And I missed him somehow—for all my looking I never
    could knock across his track.
The same with Harry, the bloke I worked with the time
    I was over upon the coast,
He went for a fly-round over to Sydney, to stay for a
    fortnight—a month at most!

He never came back, and he never wrote me—I wonder
    how blokes like him forget;
We had been where no one had been before us, we had
    starved for days in the cold and wet;
We had sunk a hundred holes that was duffers, till at
    last we came on a fairish patch,
And we worked in rags in the dead of winter while the
    ice bars hung from the frozen thatch.

Yes, them was two, and I can't help mind them—good
    mates as ever a joker had ;
But there's plenty more as I'd like to be with, for half
    of the blokes on the road is bad.
It sets me a-thinking the world seems wider, for all we
    fancy it's middling small,
When a chap like me makes friends in plenty and they
    slip away and he loses them all.

The speargrass crackles under the billy and overhead
    is the winter sun ;
There's snow on the hills, there's frost in the gully, and,
    oh, the things that I've seen and done,
The blokes that I knowed and the mates I've worked
    with, and the sprees we had in the days gone by ;
But I somehow fancy we'll all be pen-mates on the day
    when they call the Roll of the Sky.

David McKee Wright.

XLVIII.

What Used to Be.

HILL an' ridge an' barren river, all the station ridin',
Mobs o' cattle, flanks a-quiver, in the ti-tree hidin' ;
Cloudin' dust, an' red sun flarin' ; 'member how we
    caught 'em,
Wheeled 'em (thousand eyes a-glarin') ; 'long the
    sidin' brought 'em !
  Ride ! Rouse 'em up across the hill-tops !
  Bring 'em down the gullies in the dawn ;
For the boys are set an' goin', an' there's half the herd
    a-lowin'—
  Whoo-oop ! through the yellow of the dawn !

Gleamin' horns like lines o' lances — an' the mob
    stampedin' ;
Why did you—yer knew the chances—head them,
    never heedin'
Crowdin' brutes that tossed an' rolled yer—stamped yer
    inter clay ?
So I'll never more behold yer, never hear yer say—
    " Hi !   Ring 'em in along the tussock ;
    Swing 'em where the gates are set an' wide—
But the clackin' hoofs are thunder, an' ye're done if
    yer git under—
    Steady ! where the gates are yawnin' wide ! "

Wish I'd died wi' yer that mornin' when yer bed we
    made yer ;
Left yer to the night an' dawnin' with the scrub ter
    shade yer.
Yer was friend more close than brother—now ye're
    sleepin' far—
'N' I'll not ride wi' any other where the long downs are.
    Now, yer'll be ridin' in the mountings,
    Though the cattle will not turn to see yer pass ;
There's no sod or stone will hold yer when the shoutin'
    whips have told yer—
    " Ride ! the mob is breakin' in the Pass ! "

Hill an' scrub an' lone gray river — only things I'm
    lovin'—
I will serve no more for ever (Hey ! the column's
    movin',
Hear the blessed bugles blowin')—you'll be on the
    track

With the boys—them all unknowin'—bring the cattle
back.
  Ah! slow 'em down across the shingle;
  Trail 'em up the cuttin' in the dark,
There was nothin' feared or tried me wi' your knee
beside me;
  Ah-h! the crawlin' homeward in the dark!

G. B. Lancaster.

XLIX.

The Blind, Obedient Dead.

THEIR bones lie glistening on the veldt, their shoes
are rusted red,
  They are gone where spur and rifle are at rest,
Good dreams to all that legion of the blind, obedient
dead!
  Good pasture in their islands of the blest!

Knowing nothing of the combat, recking nothing if they
won
  When the echoes of the last shot died away;
They are dreaming of the far-off bush and creeks, and
shade and sun,
  And the gallops at the breaking of the day.

Did they wonder at the trumpet-call that urged them
to the onset,
  And the harder, tenser hand upon the rein,
Than the hand that held them steady for the station
roofs at sunset,
  Or the girl across a dozen miles of plain?

When the purple dusk grows deeper, and the Four
    White Stars look down,
  And an eastern wind blows oversea from home ;
To their white bones, shining silver, from the bush and
    from the town,
  Does a sigh of dear remembrance never come ?

When the mob breaks through the timber, do the
    stockmen never sigh—
  Do their hearts in idle pipe-dreams never yearn
For our horses in their long sleep where we sent them
    out to die,
  To an exile past retrieval and return ?

The girls who tingled, waiting at the slip-rails, quick to
    hear
  The ring of hoofs at moonrise through the trees—
Will they waken for a moment from their love-sleep,
    with a tear
  For the silent hoofs at rest across the seas ?

Their bones are glistening on the veldt, their shoes are
    rusted red,
  They are gone where spur and rifle are at rest.
Good dreams to all that legion of the blind, obedient
    dead !
  Good pasture in their islands of the blest !

                      M. C. Keane.

L.

A Time Will Come.

A TIME will come, a time will come,
   (Though the world will never be quite the same),
When the people sit in the summer sun,
   Watching, watching the beautiful game.

A time will come, a time will come,
   With fifteen stars in a green heaven,
Two to be batting, and two to judge,
   And round about them the fair Eleven.

A time will come, a time will come,
   When the people sit with a peaceful heart,
Watching the beautiful, beautiful game,
   That is battle and service and sport and art.

A time will come, a time will come,
   When the crowds will gaze on the game and the green,
Soberly watching the beautiful game,
   Orderly, decent, calm, serene.

The easy figures go out and in,
   The click of the bat sounds clear and well,
And over the studying, critical crowds
   Cricket will cast her witching spell.

Yet a time will come, a time will come,
   Come to us all as we watch, and seem
To be heart and soul in the beautiful game,
   When we shall remember and wistfully dream—

Dream of the boys who never were here,
　　Born in the days of evil chance,
Who never knew sport or easy days,
　　But played their game in the fields of France.

Arnold Wall.

LI.

A Leaf from a Fly-book.

THE king's road is a troublous summons calling day
　　and day ;
But my feet take the cocksfoot track—the easy, vagrant
　　way :
Beside the restless acres and the gold of noisy gorse,
The ripple lures its lover down the dazzle of its course.

Its speech is of the willow-reaches rich with lurking joy ;
The revel of the rapids where gay life is death's decoy :
My heart is with the laughing lips ; I follow up and
　　down ;
But follow not the king's white road toward the haste of
　　town.

Afoot, the wash of waders, and aloft, the haze-veiled
　　blue,—
The heart it needeth nothing so the cast fall clean and
　　true.
O carol of the running reel, O flash of mottled back !
And who will take the king's white road, and who the
　　cocksfoot track ?

The hour-glass fills with weather like a wine of slow
    content :
I throw the world behind me as a cartridge that is spent.
Then home by summer starlight bear my grass-cool,
    mottled load ;
I quit the pleasant cocksfoot track : I take the king's
    white road.

Seaforth Mackenzie.

LII.

The Song of Speed.

The engine stutters its fiery song,
   As the things of earth flash by ;
The race to the swift and the strong, and the strong,
   The turn to the sure of eye.
And death is near, but who would care ?
   For this is the death to die.

And it's oh ! for the rush of the blinding track,
   And the whirl of the leaping wheel,
The slither of foam bright overside,
   The cry of the hounds at heel.

The call of the road is a call of old
   When the song of the wind is still,
And the sunset reddens to gold, to gold
   When the poplar halts on the hill ;
But hill and road we hold them best
   As a test of the driver's skill.

And it's oh ! for the gleam of the metal ways,
    And the thunder of glowing train,
The quiver of deck to the racing screw,
    The roar of the reeling plane.

The ring of hoofs on the morning air,
    The frost-hard crunch to the ride,
Are good to hear as the distance fades,
    Eaten up by the big roan's stride ;
But the ways are best when the ways are fair
    And the throttle's open wide.

And it's oh ! for the thresh of the leeward race,
    The stretch of the bulging sail,
The curtain of dust on the level road,
    The whine of the speed-made gale.

The engine stutters its fiery song,
    As the things of earth flash by ;
The race to the swift and the strong, and the strong,
    The turn to the sure of eye.
And death is near, but who would care ?
    For this is the death to die.

                    C. Quentin Pope.

LIII.

The Pawn.

SEE how the plucky Pawn essays the fight ;
    How valiantly with double strides he goes
    Into the centre of his ardent foes,
Always straight on, save when his strokes alight

On either wing, to capture adverse Knight,
  Bishop, or Rook, or e'en the Queen oppose,
  Should she adventure her too powerful blows—
And oft prevails against her regal might.

When many brave have vanished from the field,
  The Pawn grows wary and advances slow ;
Strikes not so much, but brandishes his shield,
  To guard his King hard driven to and fro—
Sometimes he dares all that a Pawn may dare,
To win the contest at the octave square.

William M. Stenhouse.

LIV.

The Ships.

THE ships sail out, and the ships sail in,
Unfolding and folding their great white sails ;
These weary and eager the haven to win,
Those all-impatient to face the gales ;
Some sailing away to the fairy isles,
Some sailing away to the hurricane wrack ;
All sped on their way with tears and smiles.
But which will founder ! and which come back !

The ships sail in, and the ships sail out,
To the fate that is waiting by day and night ;
Though men are fearless, and ships are stout,
Though hearts are merry, and eyes are bright,
They cannot pass where the Shadow stands,
They cannot pass, though stout and brave ;
When the place is reached, they fold their hands,
And stay where the Shadow has made their grave.

E

The ships sail out, and the ships sail in,
Passing, repassing, with outspread wings ;
The anchor is tripped with a merry din,
While the careless sailor a roundelay sings ;
Some to arrive at the far-off shore,
Where love is waiting with hope and dread ;
Some to cast anchor, no more—no more—
No more, till the sea gives up its dead !

The ships sail in, and the ships sail out,
And the days go stretching away to the years ;
And men are hemmed by fate about,
We smile our smiles, and weep our tears ;
The ship-boy croons some sweet love song,
Thinking the while of his mother's face !
And the ship we thought so brave and strong,
Goes down in the night and leaves no trace !

Francis Sinclair.

LV.

Sea Prayers.

God send a shining wind to blow
Upon a little town I know
That one there strayed from sea and ships
May taste its salt upon her lips ;

That one there born of fishermen
May think on weed and rock again,
And never know the penalty
Of one who hath forgot the sea ;

That she, within that solemn town,
May treasure less the song flung down
By missel thrush and meadow lark
Than moan of gulls against the dark ;

And let the spring in her great hour,
Come with wet bud and almond flower
To wake a troubled memory
Of sails upon a windy sea.

And let this sea-child hold her hand
Forever from the servile land,
Lest she should slight infinity,
And break her faith with majesty.

God send a shining wind to blow
Upon a little town I know,
That one there born of sea and south
May know its salt upon her mouth.

Eileen Duggan.

LVI.

The Red West Road.

OFF-SHORE I hear the great propellers thunder,
   And throb and thrash so steadily and slow ;
Their booming cadence tells of seas that plunder—
Of Love's moon-seas and brave hearts thrown asunder,
   Of hot, red lips and battles, blow for blow ;
And as they sing my heart is filled with wonder,
   Though why—I scarcely know.

Perhaps it is because they tell a story,
　　And lilt a deep storm-measure as they come—
A song of old-time love and battles gory,
When men dared Hell and sailed through sunset's glory
　　With pealing trumpet tuned to rolling drum,
To hunt, and loot, and sink the jewelled quarry
　　In seas too deep to plumb.

I only know I watch the steamers going
　　Along the Red West Road, with heavy heart,
And when the night comes, look for head-lights showing,
And mark their speed—the ebb-tide or the flowing,
　　For loth am I to see them slew and start
Adown that path ; and every deep call blowing
　　Stabs like a driven dart.

The blazing West to me is always calling,
　　For in the West there burns my brightest star....
O God ! to hear the anchor-winches hauling,
And feel her speeding, soaring high and falling,
　　With steady swing across the brawling bar—
To hear the stem-struck rollers tumble sprawling,
　　And watch the lights afar.

To South and East and North the screws are singing,
　　So steadily and tunefully and slow,
But on the Western Track they thunder, flinging
Their wake afoam, and by their roar and ringing—
　　By laughter sweet, deep in my heart, I know
That down that Red West Road, with big screws
　　　　swinging,
　　Some day I'll go.

Will Lawson.

LVII.

At Sea.

When the Southern gale is blowing hard,
The watch are all on the topsail yard.

And when five come down where six went up,
There's one less to share the bite and sup.

A name is missed when the roll they call ;
A hand the less for the mainsail haul.

They steal his rags and his bag and bed ;
Little it matters to him who's dead.

Instead of the stone and carven verse,
This is his epitaph, curt and terse :

" John Smith, A.B.,
Drowned in latitude **53**,
A heavy gale and a following sea."

We have lost the way to the open sea ;
We have missed the doom we hoped to dree.

For the big ships running their easting down
Are far from the din of Sydney town.

Instead of the clean blue sunlit wave,
Our bones will lie in a darksome grave.

For the means to live we barter life.
Would I were back in the old-time strife,
Once more to be

Reefing topsails in **53**
In the blinding drift from the angry sea.

D. H. Rogers.

LVIII.

Ocean's Own.

THE song that the surf is brawling
  Is meant for their ears alone,
Who followed the deep-sea calling
  And slaved at it, blood and bone.
Oh ! softly the North Wind sings them
  A measure that bids them rest
Where Ocean, their mother, swings them
  To sleep on her throbbing breast.
The moon lifts gold in the gloaming,
  The sun in the west sinks red,
And birds of the sea pass roaming,
  But the Ocean's Own lie dead.

Perchance as they lie they're dreaming
  Of home and a childhood's tune
That rang through the storm-seas' screaming
  And sobbed in the warm monsoon ;
Or maybe again they're thrashing
  With spray on the high bridge-rail,
And labouring engines clashing
  A dirge to the men who fail.
The world passes on, forgetting,
  But, off in the ports, I know
There's many a brave heart fretting
  For the good, brave hearts laid low.

Their ships swept out on the noon-tides,
  And lonely their mast-head lights
Were quivering far, when the moon-tides
  Swam glittering through the nights ;

And strong where the storm-stars flicker
   They drove through the wash and roll,
And ever their screws spun quicker
   When baulked of their distant goal.
For the Ocean's Own were roamers—
   By power of sail and steam
They swung on the long Cape combers,
   Or droned up the Hoogli's stream.

The song that the surf is shouting
   Is meant for their ears alone
Who went to their work undoubting,
   And slaved at it, blood and bone.
Oh ! softly the Ocean swings them
   To sleep on her heaving breast,
And the wind from the sweet North sings them
   The songs that their hearts loved best.
Soft eyes are sad in their waking—
   Eyes bright with the tears unshed—
And there's many a brave heart breaking ;
   But the Ocean's Own lie dead.

                   Will Lawson.

LIX.

Homeward Bound.

THEY will take us from the moorings, they will tow us
   down the Bay,
   They will pluck us up to wind'ard when we sail.
We shall hear the keen wind whistle, we shall feel the
   sting of spray,
   When we've dropped the deep-sea pilot o'er the rail.

Then it's Johnnie heave an' start her, then it's Johnnie
     roll and go ;
   When the mates have picked the watches, there is
     little rest for Jack.
But we'll raise the good old chanty that the Homeward
     bounders know,
   For the girls have got the tow-rope, an' they're
     hauling in the slack.

In the dusty streets and dismal, through the noises of
     the town,
   We can hear the West wind humming through the
     shrouds ;
We can see the lightning leaping when the tropic suns
     go down,
   And the dapple of the shadows of the clouds.
And the salt blood dances in us, to the tune of Home-
     ward Bound,
   To the call to weary watches, to the sheet and to the
     tack.
When they bid us man the capstan how the hands will
     walk her round !—
   For the girls have got the tow-rope, an' they're
     hauling in the slack.

Through the sunshine of the tropics, round the bleak
     and dreary Horn,
   Half across the little planet lies our way.
We shall leave the land behind us like a welcome that's
     outworn
   When we see the reeling mastheads swing and sway.

Through the weather fair or stormy, in the calm and in
the gale,
  We shall heave and haul to help her, we shall hold
  her on her track,
And you'll hear the chorus rolling when the hands are
making sail,
  For the girls have got the tow-rope, an' they're
  hauling in the slack !

D. H. Rogers.

LX.

Two Voices.

To the brilliant streets and bustle of a city full of Spring,
  To the soft, contented river and the sleeping, shining
  spires,
From the distant hills disrobing there are messages
a-wing,
  From the splendid dusks and dawnings, from the
  flaming sunset fires.

I have heard them through the clamour of the people in
the sun,
  And the winds that whine at midnight when the city
  is at rest ;
And the harpstrings of my heart are set a-trembling one
by one
  Till the sweeping of their wide and keen harmonics
  calls me West.

E2

Oh ! the dew of darkling mornings on the grasses green
and grey !
Oh ! the flush before the saffron, and the blushes of
the snow !
Dark ratas stalking down the gorge (a-waiting for the
day)
To the sheen of rippling waters in the shingle sweep
below !

The threads of fire on mountain-sides in purple of the
night—
The dusted gold of tussocks and the music of the
fords—
The gorse and wattle flame that sets the dusty road
alight—
The thin, bright air—my harmony has all of these for
chords.

But from eastward comes the call of glistening beaches,
sleeping bays,
And the pale, thin, shivering grasses in the land-wind
set astir ;
And the lace of broken rollers, wove for us in summer
days,
When I sought my ocean mother with my love, and
found her fair.

Oh the beach, of worlds forsaken ! Oh the pressure
of soft hands,
In our lotus-land of ocean, lulled to mellow minor
keys !
Oh the kiss among the lupins, green among the grey of
sands,
When our swaying souls were shaken in the rush of
roaring seas !

How golden were the evenings in that slumbrous summer weather,
  When we plucked the scarlet poppies of delight and of
  desire !
How musical the mornings when we wandered forth
together !
  All royal the sea-kingdom where our feet could never
  tire.

Rival chimings, murmuring still of mountain pleasure,
sea delight,
  Mocking melodies of memories of what I loved the
  most :
When morning's golden promises have rolled away the
night,
  It is cold in this my city, and the music all is lost.

M. C. Keane.

LXI.

Sunset in the Tropics.

How grandly—when throughout the silent day,
    Some ample Day, serene, divine,
        Beneath the glowing Line
Our helpless ship had hung as in a trance
In light-blue glassiness of calm that lay
        A wide expanse
    Encircled by soft depths of ether clear,
        Whose melting azure seemed to swim
Surcharged and saturate with balmiest brilliancy—
How grandly solemn was the Day's decline !

Down as if wholly dropped from out the sky
The fallen Sun's great disc would lolling lie
Upon the narrowed Ocean's very rim,
      Awfully near !
A hush of expectation almost grim
Wrapt all the pure, blank, empty hemisphere ;
While straight across the gleaming crimson floor,
From the unmoving Ship's black burnished side,
There ran a golden pathway right into the core
Of all that throbbing splendour violet-dyed ;
Whither it seemed an easy task to follow
The liquid ripples tremblingly o'erflowing
Into the intense and blinding hollow
Of palpitating purple, showing
      The way as through an open door
Into some world of burning bliss, undreamt of hereto-
      fore.
Whose heart would not have swelled, the while
Deep adoration and delight came o'er him
At that stupendous mystery, close before him !
      Not less, but more stupendous that he knew
      Perchance, whate'er the subtle surface-play
Of Science had to teach of level ray
Reflected or refracted ; and could say,
Nay, almost count the millions to a mile,
      How far away
That pure quintessence of dark fire, deep-lying
In fathomless Flame-Oceans round him flying,
      His inconceivable circumference withdrew :
Knew all about the fringe of flames that frisk
In ruddy dance about his moon-masked face,
Set on like petals round a sunflower's disc—

Each glorious petal shooting into space
Ten times as far as Earth's vast globe is thick :
Ay ! or could prate about full many a world
Worn out, and crushed to cinders, flying fleet,
Or in cold black rotundity complete,
Into his burning bosom headlong hurled,
Just by collision to strike out fresh heat,
  And feed with flame, renew and trim,
  And keep for aye from falling dim
That monstrous and immeasurable wick—
Say rather—everlastingly keep bright
That awful mystic, God-created Light !

      Alfred Domett.

LXII.

Picton Harbour by Night.

WARM is the night and still ; the misty clouds
Obscure the moon so that there scarce is light
Left in the world ; all round, the silent hills
Sleep mystically ; and no night-haunting bird
Startles the glooming trees with mournful cry.
Silent the harbour sleeps, by myriad lights
Spread, phosphorescent, out from shore to shore—
Ripples and streaks of fire that live and die
Moment by moment, till the waters seem
Like to a sky of darkest purply-blue
Turned upside down, and thick with silver stars.

Like silver phantoms round the weedy piles
Of the dim-lighted wharf the fishes pass
In endless-seeming lines from right to left,
Ever the one direction following.   Far away,
And faint with distance, through the moonless air
The steamer's whistle sounds ; anon her lights
Shine, dim and misty, as she rounds the point,
While answering lights glare out upon the wharf.
Nearer she comes—the water 'neath her bows
Is streaked with trembling lines of green and red
And golden hues, that broad and broader grow
As on she creeps, a larger-looming form
Whose ever-throbbing engines beat and beat.

Now in her path the ghost-like silver fish—
With sound of quick and sudden little waves
Rising and flapping on a sandy shore—
Affrighted leap ; then for a moment sound
Dies all away ; and then breaks forth again
In throb of engines, shouts, and rattling chains,
And hissing steam, as to the trembling wharf
The vessel is made fast.   The flaring lamps
Flicker and flame in the soft rainy air,
And cast a glow upon the busy scene
Of loading and unloading ; silence flies
Into the darkest hollows of the hills.

Clara Singer Poynter.

LXIII.

The Mountain Spirit : A Glimpse of Mount Cook.

Saw ye a peak 'mid the ranges—
  Majestic, where peaks are high—
Cradled in billows of sombre mist
  Above where the keas fly ?
Yon is a resting-place reserved
  For kingly folk alone ;
None but the bravest feet may touch
  The Mountain Spirit's throne.

Watched ye at night o'er the ranges,
  Through Earth's remotest ways,
Like shades of far-off splendour, steal
  A nameless purple haze ?
'Tis a carpet of ether weaving,
  With restfulness replete,
Laid down where gully-ways would chafe
  The Mountain Spirit's feet.

Heard ye the North Wind chasing
  Repose from the digger's hut,
When the rumbling sluice had ceased to flow
  And the hydrant lips were shut
By the hand of icy winter ?
  Ye trembled at the noise,
Not recognizing in your dread
  The Mountain Spirit's voice.

Felt ye a deep-heart loneness
　　Come o'er ye, as winter creeps,
When twilight set on your whare-roof
　　Away from the mountain peaks ?
A longing to leave the gully,
　　In restfulness to rove
Far up the rugged heights, to share
　　The Mountain Spirit's love !

Daughters of pine-clad valleys !
　　Sons of Zealandia free,
Children of splendour !　The Spirit calls,
　　What shall your answer be ?
Yours is a home in the mountain,
　　However its peaks may rise—
For Ye are the Spirit's heirs—whose throne
　　Cloud-lapped in the ranges lies.

　　　　　　　　　　John Maclennan.

LXIV.

Onawe.

PEACEFUL it is : the long light glows and glistens
　　　　On English grass ;
Sweet are the sounds upon the ear that listens ;—
　　　　The winds that pass

Rustle the tussock, and the birds are calling,
　　　　The sea below
Murmurs, upon its beaches rising, falling,
　　　　Soft, soft, and slow —

All undisturbed the Pakeha's herds are creeping
     Along the hill ;
On lazy tides the Pakeha's sails are sleeping,
     And all is still.

Here once the mighty Atua had his dwelling
     In mystery,
And hence weird sounds were heard at midnight,
  swelling
     Across the sea.

Here once the Haka sounded ; and din of battle
     Shook the grey crags,
Triumphant shout, and agonized death-rattle
     Startled the shags.

And now such peace upon this isthmus narrow,
     With Maori blood
Once red !—these heaps of stones,—a greenstone arrow
     Rough-hewn and rude !

Gone is the Atua, and the hillsides lonely,
     The warriors dead ;
No sight, no sound ! the weird wild wailing only
     Of gull instead.

Come not the Rangitira hither roaming
     As once of yore,
To dance a ghostly Haka in the gloaming,
     And feast once more ?

Tena koe Pakeha ! within this fortification
     Grows English grass—
Tena koe ! subtle conqueror of a nation
     Doomed, doomed to pass !
               Dora Wilcox.

LXV.

Bowen Falls, Milford Sound.

O WATERFALL that fallest to the sea,
Falling for ever to white virginals
Of olden melody ! thy voice I hear
In molten moments of the summer stars
When the great sun is dead in majesty.

From the white fields of home like thee I came
Impetuous to the cliffs, and I have poured
Treasure of love on altars cold, as thou
Hast showered thy rainbow on the icy rocks,
That have not felt thy kiss—and I would die.

Athwart the hollows of the moon-fed air
Come eider tremors of thy dying plunge,
Surceasing as child-tired eyelids droop
Upon a wavy bosom, rocked with love
Poured from the heaven for ever like thy song.

The moon is kissing thy keen diadem,
Sick for her barrenness, and all her face
Creeps to thy white arc down the precipice,
As I have nestled, yearning with wild eyes,
Into the umber chancels of a soul.

Hubert Church.

LXVI.

Spring in Maoriland.

THOU wilt come with suddenness,
   Like a gull between the waves,
Or a snowdrop that doth press
   Through the white shroud on the graves;
Like a love too long withheld,
That at last has over-welled.

What if we have waited long,
   Brooding by the Southern Pole,
Where the towering icebergs throng,
   And the inky surges roll:
What can all their terror be
When thy fond winds compass thee?

They shall blow through all the land
   Fragrance of thy cloudy throne,
Underneath the rainbow spanned
   Thou wilt enter in thine own,
And the glittering earth shall shine
Where thy footstep is divine.

Hubert Church.

LXVII.

July, New Zealand.

BY fragrant tokens on the wintry way
I know she has been here, timid and fleet,
Too frail to linger yet and boldly meet
Rough Winter's jealous wrath.   Saw you her, pray?

A primrose wreath upon her brow, and gay
Red wind-flowers at her breast, all dewy-sweet,
Heard you the tread of light, wind-driven feet ?
Did such a maid delight your eyes to-day ?

Ay ! on the highway, in the windy morn,
We saw her pass, in gown of green arrayed,
With tossing hair, and sheaves of daffodils ;
But as we spied her, Winter's clam'rous horn
Mustered the storm-clouds.   Suddenly dismayed
She fled.   The grey rain hid the misty hills.

Lilla G. McKay.

LXVIII.

September, New Zealand.

ON emerald slopes the orchards break in wide,
White seas of blossom-foam ; and, as they stray,
The fragrant winds cast showers of petal-spray
Upon the grass.   Aloft in crimson pride
The rata winds its splendid bonds to hide
Bare boughs of death beneath.   So lightly sway
Long trails of clematis, frail stars of day,
Twined in a garland for a woodland bride.

The kowhai groves, in golden pageantry,
Are dulcet with the tuis' trills of mirth ;
A-down the wind the elfin clarions ring,
The dim bush echoes with wild minstrelsy,
O Life !   O Joy !   O wonder-time of earth !
September, and the ecstasy of Spring !

Lilla G. McKay.

LXIX.

At Governor's Bay.

Across the hills we went that day,
  Across the hills—oh, golden time !—
  The sea, the sky made one sweet rhyme,
And nothing could our hearts affray.

We watched the mists that wreathed soft
  The hills with mystic robes of white,
  Then slowly swelled to forms of might—
The armëd guards of vale and croft.

And gentle wind blew up the pass,
  With scent of bracken, veitch and whin,
  And lavish largesse of their kin
From broom's gold leafage shot with grass.

The blue bay slept in holy peace,
  Nor saw how clear it mirrored there
  The cliffs and islands floating near,
Awaiting the sweet day's decease.

The apple-trees had leapt to life,
  And robed in fairy sheen they stood
  In many a tiny garden rood ;
The whole wide world with joy was rife.

That one white day I saw with you
  Those beauteous things beyond the hills,
  And heard low tinklings of the rills—
That day was good.   But such are few !

Dolce A. Cabot.

LXX.
The Four Queens (Maoriland).

WELLINGTON.

HERE, where the surges of a world of sea
Break on our bastioned walls with league-long sweep,
Four fair young queens their lonely splendour keep,
Each in a city throned.   The first is she
Whose face is arrogant with empery ;
Her throne from out the wounded hill-side steep
Is rudely fashioned, and beneath her creep
The narrow streets ; and, stretching broad and free,
Like a green-waving meadow, lies the bay,
With blossom-sails and flower-wavelets flecked.
Elate she stands ; her brown and wind-blown hair
Haloes a face with virgin freshness fair,
As she receives, exuberant, erect,
The stubborn homage that her sisters pay.

DUNEDIN.

And one is fair and winsome, and her face
Is strung with winter's kisses, and is yet
With winter's tears of parting sorrow wet ;
And all her figure speaks of bonny grace.
High on the circling hills her seat has place,
Within a bower of the green bush set ;
And 'neath her feet the city slopes—a net
Of broad-built streets and green-girt garden space.
Above her high the suburbs climb to crown
Her city's battlements ; and in her thrall
Lie sleeping fiords, and forests call her queen.
About her waist she winds a belt of green,
And on her gleaming city looking down,
She hears the Siren South for ever call.

CHRISTCHURCH.

And one within a level city lies ;
To whose tree-shaded streets and squares succeeds
A vista of white roads and bordering meads,
Until each suburb in the great plain dies.
The clustering spires to crown her fair head rise,
And for a girdle round her form she leads
The Avon, green with waving river-weeds
And swept with swaying willows.   And her eyes
Are quiet with a student's reverie ;
And in the hair that clouds her dreaming face
There lurks the fragrance of some older place,
And memories awake to die again,
As, confident and careless, glad and sorrow-free
She waits, queen of the margeless golden plain.

AUCKLAND.

Set all about with walls, the last fair queen
Over a tropic city holds her sway ;
Her throne on sleeping Eden, whence through gray
And red-strewn roads and gleaming gardens green
The city wanders on, and seems to lean
To bathe her beauty in the cool, clear bay,
That out past isle and islet winds its way
To the wide ocean.   In her hair a sheen
Of sunlight lives ; her face is sweetly pale—
A queen who seems too young and maidenly,
Her beauty all too delicate and frail,
To hold a sway imperious.   But forth
From deep, dark eyes, that dreaming seem to be,
There shine the strength and passion of the North.

Arthur H. Adams.

LXXI.

The River Avon.

"Fies nobilium tu quoque fontium."—**Horace**.

I LOVE thee, Avon ! though thy banks have known
  No deed of note, thy wand'ring course along
  No bard of Avon hath poured forth in song
Thy tuneful praise ; thy modest tide hath flown
For ages on, unheeded and alone.
  I love thee for thy English name, but more
  Because my countrymen along thy shore
Have made new homes.   Therefore not all unknown
  Henceforth thy streams shall flow.   A little while
Shall see thy wastes grow lovely.   Not in vain
  Shall England's sons dwell by thee many a mile.
With verdant meads and fields of waving grain
  Thy rough, uncultured banks ere long shall smile ;
Heaven-pointing spires shall beautify thy plain.

Henry Jacobs.

LXXII.

Wellington.

RUGGED she stands, no garlands of bright flowers
Bind her swart brows, no pleasant forest shades
Mantle with twining branches her high hills,
No leaping brooks fall singing to her sea.
Hers are no meadows green, nor ordered parks ;

Not hers the gladness nor the light of song,
Nor cares she for my singing.
                 Rudely scarred
Her guardian hills encircle her pent streets,
Loud with the voices and the steps of trade ;
And in her bay the ships of east and west
Meet and cast anchor.
               Hers the pride of place
In shop and mart, no languid beauty she
Spreading her soft limbs among dreaming flowers,
But rough and strenuous, red with rudest health,
Tossing her blown hair from her eager eyes
That look afar, filled with the gleam of power,
She stands the strong queen city of the south.
                 David McKee Wright.

LXXIII.

Victoria College.

THOU shalt be greater than the city that lies
Beneath thee, though the wave curve tender foam
Athwart her beach, thou hast a fairer home
Where mountains watch thee with eternal eyes.
Within thy sanctuary men shall prize
The charm of Greece, the majesty of Rome,
And Science through thy starry-circled dome
Shall trail her robe of unimagined dyes.
As thou hast gathered round thee all that brood
Of sacrifice for knowledge, who foresee
Regeneration, humbleness, and faith
Won through the yoke of Pallas, thou shalt be
Memory for those that build thy walls when death
Had given them else forgotten solitude.
                 Hubert Church.

LXXIV.

Nelson.

BLUE foamy sea, high circling hills
   With dreaming garden squares between,
An old-world fragrance breathing soft
   Amid the waving green.

Here trade's loud wheels but slowly turn,
   Here men may pause and joy to live,
And take the seasons as they change
   With all they have to give.

Here there is room to breathe and think,
   Here there is space for souls to grow,
And life may run as pleasantly
   As Maitai's waters flow.

David McKee Wright.

LXXV.

Saturday Night.

SATURDAY night in the crowded town ;
Pleasure and pain going up and down.
Murmuring low on the ear there beat
Echoes unceasing of voice and feet.
Withered age with its load of care,
Come in this tumult of life to share,
Childhood glad in its radiance brief,
Happiest-hearted or bowed with grief,
Meet alike, as the stars look down
Week by week on the crowded town.

And in a kingdom of mystery
Rapt from this weariful world to see
Magic sights in the yellow glare,
Breathing delight in the gas-lit air,
Careless of sorrow, of grief or pain,
Two by two, again and again,
Strephon and Chloe together move
Walking in Arcady, land of love !

What are the meanings that burden all
These murmuring voices that rise and fall ?
Tragedies whispered of, secrets told,
Over the baskets of bought and sold ;
Joyous speech of the lately wed ;
Broken lamentings that name the dead :
Endless runes of the gossip's rede ;
And, gathered home with the weekly need,
Kindly greetings, as neighbours meet
There in the stir of the busy street.

Then is the glare of the gaslight ray
Gifted with potency strange to-day.
Records of time-written history
Flash into sight as each face goes by.
There as the hundreds slow moving go,
Each with his burden of joy or woe,
Souls, in the meeting of strangers' eyes
Startled this kinship to recognize,
Meet and part, as the stars look down
Week by week on the crowded town.

And still, in the midst of the busy hum,
Rapt in their dreams of delight, they come.
Heedless of sorrow, of grief, or care,
Wandering on in enchanted air,
Far from the haunting shadow of pain ;
Two by two, again and again,
Strephon and Chloe together move,
Walking in Arcady, land of love.
                    Mary Colborne-Veel.

LXXVI.
The City from the Hills.

THERE lies our city folded in the mist,
Like a great meadow in an early morn
Flinging her spears of grass up through white films,
Each with its thousand thousand-tinted globes.

Above us such an air as poets dream,
The clean and vast wing-winnowed clime of Heaven.

Each of her streets is closed with shining Alps,
Like Heaven at the end of long plain lives.
                    Arnold Wall.

LXXVII.
The City in the Plains.

IN a silvern afternoon
We saw the city sleeping,
Sleeping and rustling a little
Under the brindled hills.
Spectres of Alps behind,
Alps behind and beyond,
Tall, naked, and blue.

The city sleeps in the plain—
A flight of glittering scales
Flung in a wanton curve,
Sinking softly to earth
Flung from a Titan's palm.
In the silver afternoon
All round the shining city,
A thousand thousand sheaves
Loll in the golden plain ;
On goes the stately wain,
The dun hind striding by it,
Beside the elms and willows,
Between the Alps and the sea.

Arnold Wall.

LXXVIII.

The Street.

LONG hours the asphalt, grimed, blistered and old,
  A haggard monotone of weary gray,
    Smoulders in dull hostility.   The day
With challenging splendour, arrogant blue and gold,
Mocks at the humbled ugliness ; a bold
  Vagabond wind flings in its face his stray
  Litter of insult ; urchin dust-whirls play
Their fitful games in the gutters....But, behold—

The dusk falls, and along the purpling street
  Night strews her silence : cool and still, the air
    Enfolds the throbbing hours in a soft
Forgetfulness.   The kindly shadows meet
  In noiseless converse, and the lamps aloft
Caress with silver pavements suddenly fair.

J. H. E. Schröder.

LXXIX.

A Song of Sandhills.

I REST upon the sandhill land
  Where yellow lupins grow,
Or tangled small convolvulus
  Goes creeping strong and low ;—
A waste of yellow lupin land,
  A warm, wild land, a sandhill land,
A narrow strip of idle land
  That only idlers know !

They spade the rich, dark garden land,
  And plough the sloping hill :
They teach the busy waves to bring
  Tossed ships to harbour still.
Only the yellow lupin land,
  The sandhill land, the lazy land,—
Only the yellow lupin land
  Man has not at his will.

And joy is with the harvesters
  When stacks rise o'er the lea ;
And triumph with the fishing-boats
  Brought laden back from sea.
But no man reaps the lupin land,
  The lazy land, the lupin land ;
No man reaps the sandhill land,
  Left wild for you and me.

But in the summer shining
   The children laugh and run,
And lovers look for Arcady,
   And sick folk seek the sun,
Here in the yellow lupin land,
   The warm, dry land, the sandhill land,
The friendly strip of no-man's land
   Left wild for you and me ;
The narrow strip of lazy land
   That lies 'twixt earth and sea.

              Mary Colborne-Veel

LXXX.

Akaroa.

AT dusk in Akaroa town,
When embered sunset smoulders down
And softly wreathes the evening mist
In whorls of tender amethyst,
The air is charmed with old-world spell
Of chanting bird and chiming bell ;
And garden plots are redolent
Of poignant, unforgotten scent,
Where gillyflower and fleur de lys
Bloom underneath the cabbage tree,
And crimson rata strives to choke
With amorous arms the hoary oak,
And jonquil mocks the kowhai's gold—
Ah, sweet it is....so young, so old !

So young, so old ! So old, so new !
I wonder, at the fall of dew,
When from the evening's grey cocoon
Comes glimmering forth the moth-like moon,
And winds, upon the brooding trees,
Strum soft, nocturnal symphonies,
If kindly ghosts move up and down
In tranquil Akaroa town ;
If voyageurs from storied France
Bestride the streets of old romance,
If laughing lads and girls come yet
To dance a happy minuet ;
If grandpere muses still upon
The fortunes of Napoleon,
And grand'mere, by the walnut tree,
Sits dreaming on her rosary ?

And when, across the arch of night,
The moon wings forth in radiant flight,
Do ghostly whalers sail the bay
And ghostly crews make holiday
With ribald mirth, to drink or sup,
Or set a phantom try-pot up ?
Do shades of natives ever come
To barter pigs for nails and rum,
And dusky nymphs disport them still
About the bows of " Gange " or " Nil " ?

If so, 'tis sure they fade away
When rose and silver comes the day,
For never a phantom steals there down
To sunlit Akaroa town ;

Yet chanting bird and chiming bell
Weave something of the old-world spell,
And still in gardens there are set
The gillyflower, the mignonette,
The rata on the oak tree hung—
Ah, sweet it is....so old, so young !
The jonquil, mocking kowhai's gold—
So blithe, so new ! So triste, so old !

Mona Tracy.

LXXXI.

Silverstream.

AT Silverstream in Maoriland the hours are very young ;
   They dance to the measure that the cascades sing,
And the gay days at Silverstream are little heads hung
   Turquoise and amber, on a fine gold string.

The soft winds of Silverstream walk down the valley
   aisles
   Laden with the gorse-scent and many tui-tunes ;
They part the sweet manuka scrub and cross the
   meadow miles
   To frolic with a sea-wind tramping the dunes.

There are great hills at Silverstream, mysterious with
   trees ;
   Here and there a plume where the toi-toi nods ;
And the green hills at Silverstream are down upon
   their knees—
   Down upon their knees, girl, like great grim gods !

F

'Tis fine to feel the tall reeds against the finger-tips,
　The feet dance-dancing to the white stream's strain ;
For all the air of Silverstream puts music on the lips,
　And all the hours of Silverstream go dancing through
　　the brain.

Dancing through the brain, girl, and every strolling
　　wind
　Crooks a rounded elbow, inviting tired hands.
And the fragrance of Silverstream puts magic in the
　mind.
　The sweet winds of Silverstream lead on to magic
　　lands.

The waters of Silverstream throw lace across the
　stones—
　Silver lace and silver spray all in the silver air !
And the valley-place of Silverstream is musical with
　tones,
　Like an old Greek chorus on a moss-grown stair.

The hunched hills at Silverstream are ponderous with
　prayer,
　And the incense of Silverstream is heavy round their
　　knees ;
But the white clouds at Silverstream are twining in the
　air,
　And the swift wings at Silverstream are whirling in
　　the breeze.

White clouds and wings, girl, joyous o'er the meads,
　Slim feet and swift blood, riotous with Youth,
Take the string of gold days, tell the glowing beads,
　Where the streams and the birds chant the Litany
　　of Truth !   *Boyce Bowden.*

LXXXII.

The White Convolvulus.

THE one tall spire of the dusty town
On its beauty of circling green looked down,
Billowy foliage swelling fair,
Motionless all in the windless air.

Rising and sinking in dip and crest,
But never a movement, all at rest;
As though some mage with a curt decree,
Had said, "Be still," to a spellbound sea.

Over the leafy wave-tops high,
In the fresh, sweet air of the morning sky,
Sole speck of black in the shining day,
One hawk was winging his lazy way.

Piercing the leaves in its morning flight,
Filling the flood with a dusky light,
The sunshine fell on a river clear,
Flashing and vanishing far and near.

The rain-washed sky was a shield of blue,
The flowers ungathered, the long grass new,
For the vigour of sap and growth was rife,
Young summer hot with the wine of life.

Ranges on ranges, far crest on crest,
The long Alp-barriers closed the West,
Like the walls of the Median city old,
A guardian girdle sevenfold.

There wasted ridges looked softer through
The clinging film of their gentle blue
Where high o'er the heat-haze summits show
The cool, faint streaks of belated snow.

And all, from the mountain, the great plain o'er,
To the sickle-blade of the curving shore,
From earth below to the heaven's height,
Was a brilliance vast of the living light.

Dark as a reef by the ebb-tide stript
Heavily slumbered the eucalypt.
Laburnums, braver than lanterns bold,
Dangled their ringlets of shaking gold.

Many and many a flower maid,
For her tender beauty half afraid,
Loosed for the Lord of the Day her zone,
Seen by the wandering wind alone.

The fragile lilac had paled and fled
With the transient grace of her fragrance dead,
Brief as a vision of vanished youth,
Leaving to Summer a dream of ruth.

But the ruddy may in the hedges grew,
The satin wings of the white flag flew,
And the dandelion's common clots
Were fiery orange in wastrel plots.

The rose of poetry, poppy's prose
And wrathful peony's braggart shows
By the fretted pink and the pansy stood,
Where iris flaunted her purple hood.

Beautiful all. But we left them thus,
For the blooms of the twining convolvulus
White o'er the water as ghosts of snow,
Naiad shadows, in depths below.

Whiteness ethereal, pallor clear,
As star-beams falling on midnight mere,
As sea-foam failing when tide-waves die,
Or moonlight paling on ivory.

Lightness aerial, dew-cups swayed,
Veiling green tangle with white cascade,
While shadow-flowers seemed swung beneath
Tenderly stirred by the air's warm breath.

Greek in their beauty each chiselled cup
To its white ideal above looked up,
Through quivering labyrinths, realms that seem
A world made dim by a gliding stream.

And the milk-white bells by the river side
Between dark thicket and cool green tide
Dreamily wavered in rhythm slow
The heart-beat of music's overflow.

As the trance of fancy gives ears to hear
The stars' high music 'twixt sphere and sphere
So rarest moments in golden hours
May catch the voices of earth's frail flowers.

Faint as the sigh of a desert tree
When the wind comes wooing wistfully,
Light as the murmur of dancing flame
Voices in hush of the morning came:—

"Flowers like snow-flakes, sylphs of day,
With wind and river we swing at play,
Dancing-girls of our lord the light,
We shrink affrayed by his foe the night.

"Shuddering, dying at mortal touch,
We fade away in the spoiler's clutch,
Never in prison to droop our span,
In the heavy air of the house of man.

"But here we nod to the drowsy wind,
In tremulous hammocks of tendrils twined,
Eyeing our friends on a journey by,
The honey-drinker and dragon-fly.

"Watching them ruffle the glassy floor
Where willow tracery arches o'er,
And whispering tresses dip and rise,
Trailed in the tide as the current flies.

"Wild we are as the Maori elves
Who in looped lianas swing themselves:
Hidden fairies whose songs delight,
Wild as wild bird-notes heard in night.

"In the silent river where, mingled, dream
Unreal and real beneath the stream,
We look deep down on a sailing crew,
—Silvery clouds in the bowl of blue.

"And there we gaze at the spectral sky,
The ghost of the rocking sphere on high,
Till twilight touches, our flowers are furled,
And our shadows fold in the water-world."

William Pember Reeves.

LXXXIII.

Te Raupo.

Down in a valley,
Hemmed in by mountains,
Ripples a river
Vivid and verdant.
Foot may not ford it,
Craft may not stem it;
Which way the wind blows,
So sets its current.

Home of the old witch,
Fain she would lure thee
Down to destruction,
Whispering softly:
"Come tread my raupo,
Safe it will bear thee
O'er the morass."
Deaf to her charming,
Deaf to her wooing,
Pauses the wise man;
Ay, though each raupo
Bends in obeisance,
Whispering "Try us."

Down in the valley,
Hemmed in by mountains,
Vivid and verdant,
O'er the morass.

Bends to the East wind,
Bows to the West wind,
Wooing the stranger
To his undoing,
Raupo kakino.

M. A. Sinclair.

LXXXIV.

Mount Tarawera.

IN sunshine stretching lightly o'er
The Lake's far end from shore to shore,
Long stripes of gauze-like awning lay—
In stripes serene and white as they,
Repeated on its bright blue floor:
And many a rocky ragged bluff,
With crimson-blossoming boscage rough,
O'er beetling crest and crevice flung;—
White cliff or dark-green hill afar
With patches bleached of scarp and scar—
Stood boldly forward sunrise-fired,
Or back in sun-filled mist retired.
Untrembling, round the glistering rim
Of that expanse of blooming blue,
From headland bright or inlet's brim,
Long fringes of reflection hung.
Its ramparts stretched along the sky,
One mighty Mountain reared on high
Far o'er the rest a level crest,

With jutting rounded parapet
And rude rock-corbels rough-beset,
Half-blurred by time and tempest's fret;
While smooth its slopes came sweeping down
From that abraded cornice brown.
The mountain this, the ruddy steep,
That Ranolf, sun-awaked from sleep,
So longed to scale; and high in air
In glad imagination share
Its sky-possessing majesty
Of haughty isolation!—there
Into each dark recess to pry
And every sight and secret see
Its lofty level might reveal,
Or those grim fissures' depths conceal,
That split the Mountain into three.

About the heights, soft clouds, a few,
Clung here and there like floating flue;
Like helpless sea-birds breeze-bereft,
Unmoving spread their pinions white—
From jutting crag, deep-bathed in light,
To slip away in snowy flight;
Or closely crouched in shadowy cleft,
Like lambing ewes the flock has left.
Below, o'erjoyed at darkness fleeing,
Reviving Nature woke again
To all the exceeding bliss of being!
The minnows leapt the liquid plain
In shoals—each silvery-shivering train,
A sudden dash of sprinkled rain!

The wild-ducks' black and tiny fleet
Shot in and out their shy retreat;
The cormorant left his crowded tree
And stretched his tinselled neck for sea;
All Nature's feathered favourites poured
To their adored undoubted Lord
Of light and heat, accordance sweet
Of pure impassioned revelry;
And honey-bird and mocking-bird
And he of clearest melody,
The blossom-loving bell-bird—each
Delicious-throated devotee
In happy ignorance framed to be
Content with rapture—longing-free
For life or love they cannot reach—
Like chimes rich-tuned, to heaven preferred
The praise of their mellifluous glee;
Each lurking lyrist of the grove
With all his might sang all his love;
Till every foliage-filled ravine
And bower of amaranthine green
Rang persevering ecstasy.

Alfred Domett.

LXXXV.

Bell-birds.

THE bell-birds in the magic woods,
  Oh, hearken to the witching strain:
It flows and fills in silver floods,
  And fills and flows again.

A golden dawn, with blood-red wings,
  Flies low along the shades of night.
Oh, hearken how the carol springs,
  And trembles with delight.

The forest leaves are all afire,
  The bell-birds skim from bough to bough;
Oh, listen to the holy choir,
  So liquid and so low.

Oh, hush! oh, hear! A goblin chime,
  The dew-drop trembles on the branch;
A solo sweet, a scattered rhyme,
  A golden avalanche.

The fruits are picked, the lovely throng
  Have flown, and sung their parting strain;
But such a witchery of song
  We shall not hear again!

William Satchell.

LXXXVI.

To the Makomako, or Bell-bird
(Now rapidly dying out of our land.)

MERRY chimer, merry chimer,
  Oh, sing once more,
  Again outpour,
Like some long-applauded mimer,
  All thy vocal store.

Alas! we now but seldom hear
  Thy rich, full note
  Around us float,
For thou seem'st doomed to disappear,
  E'en from woods remote.

Some say the stranger honey-bee,
  By white men brought,
  This ill hath wrought;
It steals the honey from the tree,
  And it leaves thee naught.

The songsters of our Fatherland
  We hither bring,
  And here they sing,
Reminding of that distant strand
  Whence old mem'ries spring.

But as the old we love the new;
  Fain we'd retain
  Thy chiming strain,
Thy purple throat and olive hue:
  Yet we wish in vain.

Thy doom is fixed by Nature's law;
  Why, none can tell.
  Therefore farewell;
We'll miss thy voice from leafy shaw,
  Living silver bell.

Why should we ever know new joys,
  If thus they pass?
  Leaving, alas!
Wistful regret, which much alloys
  All that man now has.

Alexander Bathgate.

LXXXVII.

Twilight and the Makomako.

NIGHT on the forest is falling,
  Slowly the day leaves the hill,
Birds from the coverts are calling,
  Calling in tinkle and trill:

Medley of harmony ringing,
  Musical, mellow, and chiming;
Night-airs a-quiver with singing,—
  Jangle of sweetness and riming!

Twilight is gone from the hill,
  Dark are the woods to the moon;
All the sweet voices are still,
  Darkness has come too soon.—

One lone bird forgets
   That the white moon is climbing;
While over a hill a star sets,
   It is chiming and chiming:—

Bell-birds, softer than bells,
   Bell-bird, ever in tune,
What god in your bosom dwells?—
What passion your bosom swells
   As you chime to the climbing moon?

Johannes C. Andersen.

LXXXVIII.

Ti-trees and the Kukupa.

A GROVE of the southern palm
   On an islet, alone
In the bosom unrippled and calm
Of a lake with its mountain-zone:

   The wild bee's singing
Has ceased in the great white bloom;
And the once gay-scented plume
   Hangs lazily swinging:

White? it is still milk-white
   In its green top serried,
      Still milk-white,—
But drooping, heavily berried.

In the midst, iridescent and glowing,
　　Full-breasted, bead-eyed,
Bright as the Argus showing,
　　Not knowing its pride,—
(Low and gentle the call,
　　Cooing and cooing:
Wood-pigeons; that is all,
　　Cooing and wooing.)

Johannes C. Andersen.

LXXXIX.

The Riro-riro

DEAR morning, bringing sweetness like a friend
　　Whose coming grows more precious with the years,
Again to common things you lend
　　The old familiar bloom of smiles and tears.
The green fields lie unbosomed to the sun;
　　Scents of the warm wet earth are in the air;
Across the slopes the bridal hedges run;
　　And all is fresh and fair—
Roses, and gum-trees patterning the sky;
　　Kingfishers darting colour through the trees;
Blackbirds in boldness flashing by;
　　The red-roofed city coiled at ease
Around the roots of high and gracious hills;
　　And westward, far, in many a lovely fold,
The half-free country curves and flows, and fills
　　The distances with living beauty, shy and bold;

And white upon the impassive mountains' hue
  Stand little houses, shrines of human cares,
From which in softening blend of blue,
  Go little wifts of smoke like whispered prayers.

So much of beauty all around,
  But naught more dear
Than this small hidden bird's sweet sound,
  Following the changing pageant of the year
With daily note, half joy and half regret;
  Breaking the silence of the azure noon,
And heard above the volleying wind in wet
  Dark trees. As faithful as the day's own boon,
You sing your sweet sad song—and yet again,
  In rich uncounted plenitude of ease.
Ah, that refrain!
  Had it been heard by immemorial seas
Where winds that lightly kiss the storied wave
  Are odorous with petals of blown time;
And every headland is a city's grave;
  And through the silvery groves that upward climb
To broken altars, sighs the ghost of Pan—
  How bright with joy or dark with wrong
Wrought by the unquiet gods on hapless man,
  The legend men had woven round your song!

But here no cold Olympian shadows fall
  On heart or hearth, and no white altar stone
Crowns the clear hill or breaks the dark green wall
  In forest depths where no winds moan
And Quiet reigns in cool green banishment,
  Far from the fretting trouble of the world.

That is your home; there in dream-music blent
   Noon-twilight kneels at vespers; softly furled
Are all the pinions of the sun in sleep,
   And singing children of the trees
Move lightly in the columned deep,
   And charm old Silence with their melodies.
Yet here you dwell, 'mid sunlit leaves a song,
   Here where the city's tired and muddy foam
Soils the green meadows—singing sweet and long.
   Remember not that dim blue mountain home
That makes a daily wonder in the West,
   For if we trouble you with ugliness
Or weary you with dusty hot unrest,
   The bush, for all its gracious cool caress,
Holds no such love as this that overflows
   To hear your joy and pain.

As sweet as dawn, as sad as autumn rose
   Baring its fullness to the contemptuous rain,
The memories you bring from distant day:
   Youth, and the long free hours and careless mind,
The lonely deep-set homestead, worn and grey;
   The pine-wood posted on the slope behind
To take the onset of the westerlies;
   Hills blue in softness on a summer sky;
The windless orchard where the drowsy bees
   Were clover-laden, and in grasses high
Under the old untended trees we found
   The warm ripe fruit; and idly led,
Watched some cloud galleon westward bound
   Sweep proudly by the purple mountain head;
Or travelled in some old delicious tale
   Down the long ecstasy of afternoon.

Dear singer, you were there, and in the vale
  Where dropped the clear cool stream in laugh and
      croon
From ledge to ledge, or incantations made
  In dark unholy tunnellings
Under the arch of interlaced shade—
  Your singing swelled romance's murmurings;
Or on the dark verandah, long and deep,
  By dolichos and honeysuckle walled,
We watched the summer evening's sadness creep
  O'er sea and land; hid wekas called
In harsh monotony, and, landward sped,
  Black swans in phalanx drove across the sky;
Seaward the tumbling bar and bluff-brow'd head
  Were slowly blurred, and with its whispering sigh
The evening land wind stirred the darkening trees.
  O warm and sweet and heavy-scented night,
Where mingled in the haunts of quiet and ease,
  Native and far-borne perfumes of delight—
Roses and stocks with rapture tremulous,
  Pale gilly-flowers in exiled loveliness,
Verbenas and magnolias odorous;
  And stealing o'er these, like a soft caress,
Cool scents from wide white-flecked manuka lands,
  The bush's rotten-sweet fertility,
Mixed with the breath of tide-embracing sands,
  The sharp, salt, thrilling presence of the sea.
And you, singing the well-loved day to sleep,
  Shook music from some Paradise apart,
Then stirred some hitherto unmoved deep,
  And heaven blossomed in the grateful heart.

Befriend me, singer, when the last dear day
  To this old lover smiles her sad farewell,
And senses quickening when they cannot stay
  Are tuned to unheard whispers of her spell.
Sing me again of beauty, how she led
  Youth wild with dreams; and in the press of life
Trailed with her light-foot tread
  High-walled, rest-charméd gardens, closed to strife.
Beauty that glistens like a dew-drenched rose,
  Lovely and frail against the eternal sky,
Beauty that is alive with joy, but knows
  The searching sadness of mortality.
The holier part of beauty this—
  To tremble at the brimming sense of doom,
To taste regret upon the lips of bliss,
  And start a ghost within the guarded room.
So, in my quiet passing let me hear
  The invocation I have loved so long,
That I may carry with me, sweet and clear,
  The knowledge that your song
To those who follow after will be one
  With beauty, and, as I have seen,
So will they marvel in the living sun,
  And cherish the delight of what has been.

                                    Alan E. Mulgan.

XC.

Two Sonnets.

1. THE NIGHTINGALE.

LAST eve I heard an English nightingale
   Pouring her very soul out to the sky,
   When nothing moved save Solitude and I
Pacing the fields together till the pale
Enchanted moonlight flooded all the vale.
   And she sang on, and high and yet more high
   Toward Heaven thrilled that rich and passionate cry,
Till at the full it seemed to flag and fail.

Thou art the embodied Spirit of the Past,
   O Nightingale! thou singest Love and Sorrow
For all that was, for all that could not last,
   Being too perfect; never shall to-morrow
Assuage thy pain, nor ever grant relief
For thy superb and all-consuming grief.

2. THE BELL-BIRD.

Not so thou carollest at break of day,
   O Bell-bird! when the world is flushed with light
   And slips triumphant from the clasp of night,
And the wind wakes and blows the clouds away,
And the hill-spirits rise and shout at play,
   Rejoicing. Then thou takest sudden flight
   From tree to tree, and warblest with delight,
Thou and thy comrades jubilant and gay!

Thou singest of the Future, radiant Bird!
 Surely the Gods have lent thee sacred fire
And taught thee songs forgotten or unheard
 By old-world men! thou singest of Desire,
Youth, and high Hope, and the infinity
Of all we dream the Newer Worlds may be.

Dora Wilcox.

XCI.

The Legend of Papa and Rangi.

THERE was NIGHT at the first—the great Darkness.
 Then PAPA, the Earth ever genial, general Mother,
And our Father, fair RANGI—the Sky—in commixture
 unbounded confusedly clave to each other;
And between them close cramped lay their children
 gigantic—all Gods. He the mightiest, eldest, the
 Moulder
And Maker of Man—whose delight is in heroes—
 TUMATAU — the Courage-inspirer, the Battle-
 upholder;
TANGAROA, far-foaming, the Sire of the myriads that
 silvery cleave the cerulean waters;
And the solemn and beauteous TANE, who gathers
 his stateliest, ever-green, tress-waving daughters
Into forests, the sunny, the songster-bethridden; then
 RONGO—the peaceful, the kindly provider
Of the roots that with culture are milkiest, pithiest;
 he too, who flings them in wider and wider

Profusion uncultured, nor needing it—HAUMIA; lastly,
  the fiercest of any, the Rider
Of Tempests—TAWHIRI, joy-wild when his sons—
  when the Winds multitudinous rush with the rattle
Of hail and the sting of sharp showers and the hurry
  of turbulent clouds to aerial battle.
All these did the weight of vast Rangi o'erwhelm;
  there restlessly, rampantly, brother on brother
Lay writhing and wrestling in vain to get free from
  the infinite coil and confusion and smother;
Till the forest-God, Tane, with one mighty wrench
  irresistible prized his great parents asunder—
With his knotty and numberless talons held down—
  held the Earth and its mountain magnificence under,
Heaved the Heavens aloft with a million broad limbs
  shot on high, all together rebounding, resilient:
Then at once came the LIGHT interfused, interflowing
  —serenely soft-eddying, crystalline—brilliant!—
Now the Sons all remained with the Earth but Tawhiri;
  he, sole, in tempestuous resentment receding
Swept away at the skirts of his Father—the Sky; but
  swiftly to vengeance and victory leading
His livid battalions, returned in his terrors, his kindred
  with torment and torture to harry:
Tangaroa rolled howling before him—even Tane
  bowed down; could his blast-besplit progeny parry
His blows, or withstand the full pelt of his torrents
  that flung them o'er wastes of white Ocean to
  welter?
Could Rongo do more e'er he fled than conceal in the
  warmth of Earth's bosom his children for shelter?—

No! they shrank from the Storm-God amazed and
    affrighted. One brother—Tumatau—alone durst
    abide him,
Tumatau and Man stood before him unswerving,
    deserted by all, disregarded, defied him!
But Man that defection still punishes daily; with
    snare, net and spear still their offspring he chases,
Tangaroa's and Tane's—the feathered—the finny; still
    turns up and tears from her tender embraces
All that Rongo has laid in the lap of his Mother;
    while fiercely Tawhiri still plagues *all* their races—
Ever wreaks his wild anger on blue Tangaroa, and
    whirls into spray-wreaths the billows he lashes—
On the Earth whose rich berries and blossoms he
    scatters and scathes; on the forests he splinters and
    crashes;
And on Man who stands firm when his thunder is
    loudest and laughs when his lightning incessantly
    flashes!

                    Alfred Domett.

XCII.

Rona.

Rona, Rona, sister olden,—
    Rona in the moon!
You'll never break your prison golden,—
    Never, late or soon!

Rona, for her crying daughter,
    At the dead of night
Took the gourd and went for water,—
    Went without a light.

There she heard the owlets wrangle
  With an angry hoot:
Stick and stone and thorny tangle
  Wounded Rona's foot.

"Boil the moon!" she said in passion;
  "Boil your lazy head!
Hiding thus in idle fashion
  In your starry bed!"

Angry was the moon in heaven;
  Down to earth she came:—
"Stay you ever unforgiven
  For the word of shame!

Up!—You made the moon a byword—
  Up and dwell with me!"
Rona felt the drawing skyward,—
  Seized a ngaio tree.

But from earth the ngaio parted
  Like a bitten thread:
Like a comet, upward darted
  Rona overhead.

In the moon is Rona sitting,
  Never to be free;
With the gourd she held in flitting,
  And the ngaio tree.

Rona and the moon together
  Wage unending strife:
Deep in the abysses nether
  One had yielded life,

But for it, the Lake of Heaven,
  Great Waiora cool;
Where they wash for evens seven
  In the crystal pool.

There Waiora's living waters
  Purge the battle stain;
There the ancient angry daughters
  Lave and grow again.

You'll never break the prison golden,—
  Never, late or soon,
Rona, Rona, sister olden,—
  Rona in the moon!

Jessie Mackay.

XCIII.

New Zealand.

. . . . . Still alive is that Fish!
Here, on the edge of the world, on the rim of the
    morning,
She stands, Tangaroa's dear daughter, a vigorous
    virgin,
Fresh from the foam.
Still the daylight is young in her eyelids, and on her
    full forehead;
Her brown limbs gleam from the bath,
Dew is yet in her wind-tossing hair.

The wild winds are her walls, and she stands here,
    untamed as sea-water,
Brave with the heart of the Ocean, sweet with the
    heart of the Sun.
Ay!
A sea-wind for freshness, a sea-wave for brightness,
A sea-sunrise for beauty, a strong sea for strength,
Here she stands, Maui's Fish, here she shines, a new
    Land from the Ocean,
Alive, 'mid the ever-live Sea.

Alive! Yea, Te Ika—
Of the Bone of the Past, of the Blood of the Present,
Here, at the end of the earth, in the first of the
    Future,
Thou standest, courageous and youthful, a country to
    come!
Lo, thou art not defiled with the dust of the Dead,
    nor beclouded with thick clouds of Custom:
But, springs and quick sources of life all about thee,
    within thee,
Splendid with freshness, radiant with vigour, con-
    spicuous with hope,
Like a beacon thou beckonest back o'er the waters,
    away o'er the world:
The while, looking ahead with clear eyes,
Like Maui, thou laugh'st, full of life!

And do not regard overmuch
Those tedious old Brothers, that still must be
    pribbling and prabbling about thee
(Paddlers inshore: when a Maui has fish'd, then they
    claim the canoe!) . . .

Laugh at them, Land!
They are old: are they therefore so wise?
Thou art young, Te Ika: be young!
Thou art new: be thou new!
With keen sight, with fresh forces, appraise those old
    grounds of their vaunting,
Dip in deep dew of thy seas what swims yet of their
    catch, and renew it,—
The rest, fish very long caught,
Toss it to them!
And address thee to catches to come.
Rich hauls to bold fishers, new sights to new sight, a
    new world to new eyes,
To discoverers, discoveries! Yea,
Offspring of Maui! recall the experience of Maui.
A dead fish he did not receive it? No, No!
He endured, he adventured, he went forth, he
    experimented,
He found and he fetch'd it, alive!

Yea, alive! a Fish to give thanks for.
Ah, ah, Tangaroa, well done!
Thou livest, Te Ika a Maui!
Enough! My last word:—
Live! Dare! Be alive!

B. E. Baughan.

XCIV.

The Coming of Te Rauparaha.

BLUE, the wreaths of smoke, like drooping banners
From the flaming battlements of sunset
Hung suspended; and within his whare
Hipe, last of Ngatiraukawa's chieftains,
Lay a-dying! Ringed about his death-bed,
Like a palisade of carven figures,
Stood the silent people of the village—
Warriors and women of his hapu—
Waiting. Then a sudden spilth of sunlight
Splashed upon the mountain-peak above them,
And it blossomed redly like a rata.

With his people and the twilight pausing;
Withering to death in regal patience,
Taciturn and grim, lay Hipe dying.

Shuddering and green, a little lizard
Made a ripple through the whare's darkness,
Writhing close to Hipe! Then a whisper
On the women's dry lips hesitated
As the ring of figures fluttered backwards;
" 'Tis the Spirit-Thing that comes to carry
Hipe's tardy soul across the waters
To the world of stars!" And Hipe, grimly,
Felt its hungry eyes a-glitter on him;
Then he knew the spirit-world had called him;
Knew the lizard-messenger must hasten,
And would carry back a soul for answer.

Twenty days in silence he had listened,
Dumb with thoughts of death, and sorely troubled
For his tribe left leaderless and lonely.

Now like sullen thunder from the blackness
Of the whare swept a voice untinctured
With a stain of sickness; and the women,
Breaking backwards, shrieked in sudden terror,
" 'Tis the weird Thing's voice, the greenish lizard,
All-impatient for the soul of Hipe!"
But the warriors in the shadow straightened
Drooping shoulders, gripped their greenstone meres,
And the rhythmic tumult of the war-dance
Swept the great pah with its throbbing thunder:
While their glad throats chanted, "E, 'tis Hipe!
Hipe's voice that led us in the battle;
Hipe, young, come back to lead us ever!"

"Warriors and women of my hapu,"
Whirled the voice of Hipe from the darkness,
"I have had communion with the spirits;
Listen while I chant the song they taught me!

"I have seen the coming end of all things,
Seen the Maori shattered 'neath the onrush
Of the white-faced strangers. Like the flashing
Of the Sun-God through the ranks of darkness,
Like the Fire-God rippling through the forest,
Like the winter's silent blight of snowflakes—
Lo! the strange outbreak of pallid blossoms—
Sweeps this surging wave of stranger-faces,
Frothing irresistibly upon us.

"Lo, the Pakeha shall come and conquer;
We have failed; the Gods are angry with us.
See, the withered autumn of our greatness!

"Old ancestral myths and sacred legends
That we deemed immortal—(priest and wizard
Died, and yet their stories, like a river,
Through the long years ran on, ever changeless!)—
Shall be buried; and the names long given
To each hill, and stream, and path and gully,
Shall be like a yesterday forgotten,
Blown like trembling froth before the sea-breeze.

"And the gods that people all our islands—
This great sea of presences immortal,
Living, real, alert for charm or evil,
Hurrying in every breeze, and haunting,
Heavy-winged, the vistas of the forest,
Deluging the daylight with their presence,
Teeming, flooding, brimming in the shadows—
Shall be banished to their spirit-regions,
And the world be lorn of gods and lonely.

"And the Maori shall no long time linger
Ere, a tardy exile, he shall journey
To the under-world. Yet he shall never
Break before this influx, but shall fight on
Till, a mangled thing, the tide o'erwhelm him.
And my tribe, the mighty Ngatiraukawa,
Had they left one worthy chieftain only
Who could lead my people on to victory,
Who could follow where my feet have trodden,

Might yet rear their name into a pillar
Carved with fame, until their stubborn story
From the mists of legend broke tremendous,
Flaming through the chilly years to follow
With a sunset-splendour, huge, heroic!" . . .

So he ceased, and tremulous the silence
Sighed to voice in one long wail of sorrow.
So; it was the truth that Hipe taught them:
None was left to lead them on to victory;
None could follow where his feet had trodden.

Then by name old Hipe called the chieftains—
Weakling sons of that gaunt wrinkled giant,
Stunted saplings blanching in the shadow
Of the old tree's overarching greatness.
One by one he called them, and they shivered,
For they knew no answer to his question,
"Can you lead my people on to victory?
Can you follow where my feet have trodden?" . . .

Then the old chief in his anger chanted
Frenziedly a song of scorn of all things,
And the frightened people of the village—
Warriors and women of his hapu—
Quavered into murmurs 'neath the whirlwind
Of his lashing words; and then he fretted
Into gusts of anger; and the lizard
Made a greenish ripple in the darkness,
Shuddering closer to him. And the people
Bending heard a whisper pass above them,
"Is there none to lead you on to victory,
None to follow where my feet have trodden?"

Lo, a sudden rumour from the edges
Of the silent concourse, where the humblest
Of the village couched in utter baseness—
There among the outcasts one leapt upright,
Clean-limbed, straight and comely as a sunbeam,
Eager muscles clad in tawny velvet,
Eyes aflash with prescience of his power,
Yet a boy, untried in warriors' warfare,
Virgin to the battle! And untroubled
Rang a daring voice across the darkness,
"Yes, my people, one there is to lead you;
I dare point you on to fame and victory,
I dare tread where Hipe's feet have trodden.
Yea," and prouder sang the voice above them,
"I can promise mightier fame unending;
I shall lead where Hipe dared not tempt you;
I shall make new footprints through the future—
I, the youth Te Rauparaha, have spoken!"

On the boy who braved them stormed the people,
Swept with fear and anger, and they clamoured,
"Who so proudly speaks, though not a chieftain?
Rank and name and fame he has none; how then
Dare he lead when sons of chieftains falter?"

But the boy leapt forward to the whare,
Clean-limbed, straight and comely as a sunbeam,
Eager muscles clad in tawny velvet,
Eyes aflash with prescience of his power,
Swinging high the mere he had fashioned
Out of wood, and carven like a chieftain's—
Ay, and with the toy had slain a foeman!

Flinging fiery speech out like a hailstorm,
"If ye choose me chieftain I shall lead you
Down to meet the white one on the sea-coast,
Where his hordes shall break like scattered billows
From our wall of meres. Him o'erwhelming,

"I shall wrest his flaming weapons from him,
Fortify for pah the rugged island
Kapiti; then like a black-hawk swooping
I shall whirl upon the Southern Island,
Sweep it with my name as with a tempest,
Overrun it like the play of sunlight,
Sigh across it like a flame, till Terror
Runs before me shrieking! And our pathway
Shall be sullen red with flames and bloodshed,
And shall moan with massacre and battle!

"Quenching every foe, beneath my mana
Tribe shall stand with tribe, till all my nation
Like a harsh impassive wall of forest
Imperturbably shall front the strangers. . . .

"Then the name of me, Te Rauparaha,
And the tribe I lead, the Ngatitoa,
Shall be shrined in sacred myth and legend
With the glamour of our oft-told prowess
Wreathed about them! Think, we shall be saviours
Of a race, a nation! And this island
We have sown so thick with names—each hillock,
Glen and gully, stream and tribal limit—
Shall for ever blossom like a garden
With the liquid softness of their music!
And the flute shall still across the evening
Lilt and waver, brimming with love's yearning!" . . .

Hipe heard, and, dying, cried in triumph,
"Warriors and women of my hapu,
He shall lead you, he, Te Rauparaha!
He shall do the things that he has promised.
He may fail; but think how grand his failure!
He alone can lift against the tempest
That proud head of his, and hugely daring,
God-like, hugely fail, or hugely conquer!"

Still he spoke, but suddenly the lizard
Made a greenish ripple through the darkness,
And was gone! Upon the long lone journey
To Te Reinga and the world of spirits
It had started with the soul of Hipe!

Then the plaintive wailing of the women
Quavered through the darkness, and a shudder
Took the slaves that in a horror waited
For the mercy of the blow to send them—
Ah! the sombre, slowly-stepping phalanx—
To the twilight world with Hipe's spirit.

Arthur H. Adams.

XCV.

Passages from
" The March of Te Rauparaha."

RAUPARAHA's war chant,
Rauparaha's fame-song,
Rauparaha's story
Told on the harp-strings,
Pakeha harp-chords
Tuned by the stranger.

.   .   .   .   .   .

Moan the waves,
Moan the waves,
Moan the waves as they wash Tainui,
Moan the waves of dark Kawhia,
Moan the winds as they sweep the gorges,
Wafting the sad laments and wailings
Of the spirits that haunt the mountains—
Warrior souls, whose skeletons slumber
Down in the caverns, lonely and dreary,
Under the feet of the fierce volcano,
Under the slopes of the Awaroa!
Moan the winds,
Moan the winds,
Moan the winds, and waves, and waters,
Moan they over the ages vanished,
Moan they over the tombs of heroes,
Moan they over the mighty chieftains
Sprung from giants of far Hawaiki!
Moan they over the bones of Raka,

Moan they over the Rangatira
Toa, who founded the Ngatitoa!
Moan they over Wera Wera,
  Sire of him,
  Sire of him,
Sire of him they called Te Rauparaha!
Echoes of the craggy reeks,
Echoes of the rocky peaks,
 Echoes of the gloomy caves,
 Echoes of the moaning waves,
Echoes of the gorges deep,
Echoes of the winds that sweep
O'er Pirongia's summit steep,
 Chant the Rangatira's praise,
 Chant it in a thousand lays,
Chant the Rangatira's fame,
Chant the Rangatira's name,
 Te Rauparaha, Te Rauparaha!

Sound his praises far and near,
For his spirit still is here
 Flying through the gusty shocks,
 When the sea-ghosts climb the rocks
Clad in foam shrouds, thick and pale,
Woven by the howling gale
 In the ocean's monster loom!
 Warp of green and weft of gloom
Woven into sheets of white
By the wizards of the night;
Chant his name each ocean sprite,
 Te Rauparaha, Te Rauparaha!

"The sea rushed up with plunging shocks,
  Kapai! Rauparaha!
To claim the land and beat the rocks,
  Kapai! Rauparaha!
The rocks stood firm and broke the waves;
So stood the Ngatitoa braves—
Ngatitoa's foes are slaves,
  Kapai! Rauparaha!

"The stars came out to match the sun,
  Kapai! Rauparaha!
To claim the crown that he had won,
  Kapai! Rauparaha!
The sun shot forth its brightest rays,
And quenched the stars in fiery blaze;
Then chant the Ngatitoa's praise,
  Kapai! Rauparaha!

"The Tuis came the Hawk to kill,
  Kapai! Rauparaha!
And yet the Hawk is living still,
  Kapai! Rauparaha!
The Hawk can soar, the Hawk can fight—
The Tuis tried to stay his flight—
The Hawk shall have a feast to-night,
  Kapai! Rauparaha!

. . . . . .

"Slaves should have but little words,
  Kapai! Rauparaha!
Little songs for little birds,
  Kapai! Rauparaha!

Little Tuis should not try
With their little wings to fly
Where the Hawk is perched on high,
    Kapai! Rauparaha!"

           Thomas Bracken.

XCVI.

The Last Haka.

AND then they danced their last war-dance to gain
The physical fever of the blood and brain
That might their dashed and drooping spirit sustain,
Nor let their flagging courage fail or flinch.
Then formal frenzy in full play was seen;
The dancers seemed a mob of maniacs, swayed
By one insane volition, all obeyed,
Their mad gesticulations to enact
With frantic uniformity, exact
As some innumerably-limbed machine,
With rows of corresponding joints compact
All one way working from a single winch:
The leaping, dense, conglomerate mass of men
Now all together off the ground—in air—
Like some vast bird a moment's space—and then
Down, with a single ponderous shock, again
Down, thundering on the groaning, trembling plain!
And every gesture fury could devise
And practice regulate was rampant there;
The loud slaps sounding on five hundred thighs;

Five hundred hideous faces drawn aside,
Distorted with one paroxysm wide;
Five hundred tongues like one, protruding red,
Thrust straining out to taunt, defy, deride;
And the cold glitter of a thousand eyes
Upturning white far back into the head;
The heads from side to side with scorn all jerking
And demon-spite, as if the wearers tried
To jerk them off those frantic bodies working
With such convulsive energy the while!
—Thus—and with grinding, gnashing teeth, and fierce
Explosions deep in oft narrated style,
Those volleyed pants of heartfelt execration;
Or showers of shuddering, hissing groans that pierce
The air with harsh accordance, like the crash
When regiments their returning ramrods dash
Sharp down the barrel-grooves with quivering clang
In myriad-ringing unison—they lash
Their maddened souls to madder desperation!—
Thus all the day their fury hissed and rang;
So groaned, leapt, foamed, grimaced they o'er and o'er;
Till all were burning, ere the Sun should soar,
Against that stubborn Fort to fling themselves once
    more.

Alfred Domett.

XCVII.

The Curse of Tuhotu.

WOE to the seekers of pleasure!
  Woe to the Maori race!
  Woe to this time and place!
For filled is the wrathful measure,
  And Vengeance cometh apace;
  Only a little space,
And a man will give all his treasure
  To be hid from the angry face
Of a justly-incensed God!
The earth shall quake at His nod,
And the hills dissolve in fire
Before His enkindled ire!

Woe to Wairoa the gay!
I see her at close of day,
  Go like a child to sleep;
I see her, ere morning breaks,
Wake, as a madman wakes
  From a dream of the nethermost deep!

The earth is rent asunder,
  The heavens are black as a pall;
  The bright flames rise and fall;
Deep rumblings come from under,
  While high in air,
  'Mid the lightning's glare,
Bellows the angry thunder!
  Wairoa is gone—is fled—
  The wicked ones all are dead!

Woe to Ariki the proud!
  Humbled shall be her pride.
  She smiles on the fair hill-side:
But I see the gathering cloud—
I hear the mutterings loud.
O God! the cloud has burst!
  In a rain of living fire
  I see Ariki expire,
By sloth and sin accurst!

Woe unto Moura, woe!
  She is dreaming of peace and rest,
  Like a bird in its quiet nest,
While the blue lake lies below.
  Her sons to folly wander;
  The stranger's gold they claim;
  To the stranger's vice they pander—
  They sell her daughters' shame!
  God stamps His foot in anger,
  The earth's foundations shake:
    For Moura weep,
    She lieth deep
  In Tarawera's lake!

Waitangi, thy waters of wailing
Are lamenting, unavailing,
  Too late to avert thy doom!
Too late doth thy conscience waken,
For, in sin and shame o'ertaken,
  Thy glory shall sink in gloom!
    Mourn, ye weeping waters,
    The fate of your sons and daughters
  Who sleep in a nameless tomb!

Deep and eternal shame,
   Bitter and endless woe,
To each tribe of ancient name!
They shall perish in vengeful flame,
   And sink to the realm of Po!
Weep, Ngatitoi, Tuhourangi,
Weep for Wairoa, Waitangi,
   Ariki, and Moura the fair;
They have drunk of the wine of Pleasure,
And now they must drain a measure
   Of Sorrow and dire Despair;
They have heard with scoffs and scorning
The voice of solemn warning;
   God striketh, and will not spare!

                              John Liddell Kelly.

XCVIII.

The Lament for Mōrérē.

*(Tamati Honé's chant of mourning for his sons and
   tribesmen killed in battle at Sentry Hill, Taranaki,
   1864.)*

[TRANSLATION]

THE lightning flashed, the thunder crashed
   On Turamoé hill,
Portent of battle, death and woe,
Omen that boded forth thy fall,
   O Tiopira!
Thou who stood'st nobly forth
In the bows of the canoe!

And thou, Hāpeta! Cold thou liest!
Death spread his lure for thee;
The dragon of the cave
    Was loosed on thee.

.   .   .   .

Ah me, my sons!
My flock of happy forest-birds,
That flew from tree to tree in brighter days—
Now fast in woodsman's snare.
My beautiful, my slender totara,
Snapped by the wintry gale!
My tall red-painted warrior band,
How grand ye dashed upon the foe!
And I—I saw ye go;
I, too, rushed naked to the fight,
    O sons—at Mōrērē!

.   .   .   .

O heroes of my house! How grand
    That charge
Above Whakaahurangi's woods that day!
Lonely I lie within my home
Beside Kapuni's river-mouth,
And cherish bitter thoughts and ever weep—
    My sons!

.   .   .   .

Lofty and lone stands Taranaki
    In the West;
So tall and splendid thou, O Kingi—
    And now thou'rt gone!

Still o'er the forests, still above the clouds
    Towers Taranaki;
But Kingi's gone—foremost in council,
    Foremost in the fight.
I searched the reddened field, I found him dead
    At Mōrérē!

    .   .   .   .   .

    O restless sea,
Beating for ever on the sounding sands
Below the cliffs of Wharau—
Like thee for ever I'll lament!
Oh son, arise! Return, return!
Cannot thy prophet make thee live again—
Restore thy breath, and bind thy wounds?
    Ah me—my hopes!

    .   .   .   .   .

The billows from the west roll in
And thundering crash on 'Taraimaka's shore—
There, too, my children fought
And red-eyed, furious, leaped in battle dance.
On lone Mōrérē's hill they fell;
There broken lay my tribe!
O simple ones and brave,
Entrapped in Whiro's snare—
    The snare of Fate!
Ye charged along the path of Death;
Ye were deceived—
Beguiled in that false path,
The path of Hau!

    .   .   .   .   .

How vain your valour, vain your charge
    Against Mōrérè's walls!
Wrecked on that rocky coast of death
    Are all my crews—
Tainui, Tokomaru, Kurahaupo, Aotea—
Ah me! my brave canoes
Lie shattered on the shore!

                       James Cowan.

XCIX.

The Noosing of the Sun-God.

    "TIRAHA, Te Ra!
     I am Maui,—
Maui the bantling, the darling;—
Maui the fire-thief, the jester;—
Maui the world's fisherman!
I am Maui, man's champion!
    Thou art the Sun-God,
Te Ra of the flaming hair.
Heretofore man is thy moth.
What is the life of man,
Bound to thy rushing wings,
Thou fire-bird of Rangi?
A birth in a burning;
A flash and a war-word;
A failing, a falling
Of ash to the ashes
Of bottomless Po!

I am Maui!
The great one, the little one;
A bird that could nest
In the hand of a woman.
I—I have vanquished
The Timeless, the Ancients.
The heavens cannot bind me,
But I shall bind thee.
    Tiraha, Te Ra!"

    Ah, the red day
Of the fighting of Maui!
How he waxed, how he grew:
How the Earth Mother shook!
And the sea was afraid,
And receded and moaned
Like a babe that is chidden.
The rope that was spun
In the White World of Maui
With blessing and cursing
Curled on the dazzling
    Neck of Te Ra.

"A pull for the living
That gasp in the light!
A pull for the dead
In abysses of Po!
A pull for the babes
That are not, but shall be
In the cool, in the dawn,
In the calm of Hereafter!
    Tiraha, Te Ra!"

The sky was a smother
Of flame and commotion.
Low leaped the red fringes
To harass the mountains.
And Maui laughed out:—
"Hu, hu, the feathers
Of the fire-bird of Rangi!"
But the rope of the blessing,
The rope of the cursing,
It shrivelled and broke.
He stooped to the coils
And he twisted them thrice,
And thickly he threw it
On the neck of Te Ra.

"Twice for the living!
And twice for the dead!
And twice for the long Hereafter!"
All the heart of the heavens,
The heart of the earth,
Hung on the rope of Maui.
But the red lizards licked it;
The fire-knives chipped it;
It frittered and broke.
Then Maui stood forth
On the moaning headlands
And looked up to Io—
Io, the Nameless, the Father,
To whom the eyes pray,
But whom the tongue names not.
And a thin voice clave the fire
As the young moon cleaves the blue
Like a shark's tooth in the heavens.

"O my son, my son, and why are thy hands so red?
  Wilt fight the fire with fire, or bind the Eterne
    with deeds?
Shatter the strong with strength?—Nay, like to unlike
    is wed:
  What man goes to the river to smite a reed with
    reeds?

"Soft and wan is water, yet it is stronger than fire:
  Pale and poor is patience, yet it is stronger than
    pride.
Out of the uttermost weakness cometh the heart's
    desire:
  Thou shalt bind the Eternal with need and naught
    beside.

"Plait thee a rope of rays, twist thee a cord of light:
  Twine thee a tender thread that never was bought
    nor sold:
Twine thee a living thread of sorrow and ruth and
    right,
  And were there twenty suns in Rangi, the rope
    shall hold."

        Then Maui bowed his head
        And smote his palms together.—
        "Ina, my sister, little one, heed!
          Give me thy hair."

        Ina, the Maiden of Light,
          Gave him her hair.
        Swiftly he wove it,
        Laughing out to the skies:—
        "Thrice for the living!
        Thrice for the dead!
        And thrice for the long Hereafter!"

The thin little cord
Flew fast on the wind
Past the Eyes of the Kings
To the neck of Te Ra.
And then was the pull.
The red lizards licked it;
The fire-knives chipped it;
But it stood, but it held.
And measured and slow
Evermore was the flight
Of the fire-bird of Rangi.

Jessie Mackay.

c.

The Lost Tribe.

Not always do they perish by the sword
  Who by the sword have lived. A harder fate,
  A direr doom, an end more desolate
Befel the remnant of one warlike horde!

Ngatimamoe! From your Chiefs a word
  Was wont to summon all the woes that wait
  On warfare—plunder, slaughter, lust and hate;
You then were feared; your name is now abhorr'd!

Driven to the wild, inhospitable West,
  The strong tribe dwindled; mother, sire and son
    Fought Cold and Famine—foes that ne'er relented.
The last child starved at the last mother's breast,
  The last stern warrior laid him down alone,
    Unsepulchred, unhonoured, unlamented!

John Liddell Kelly.

CI.

Miroa's Song.

ALAS, and well-a-day! they are talking of me still:
By the tingling of my nostril, I fear they are talking
ill;
Poor hapless I—poor little I—so many mouths to fill,
    And all for this strange feeling, O this sad sweet
    pain!

O senseless heart—O simple! to yearn so and to pine
For one so far above me, confest o'er all to shine—
For one a hundred dote upon, who never can be mine!
    O 'tis a foolish feeling—all this fond sweet pain!

When I was quite a child—not so many moons ago—
A happy little maiden—O then it was not so;
Like a sunny-dancing wavelet then I sparkled to and
    fro;
    And I never had this feeling, O this sad sweet pain!

I think it must be owing to the idle life I lead
In the dreamy house for ever that this new bosom-weed
Has sprouted up and spread its shoots till it troubles
    me indeed
    With a restless weary feeling—such a sad sweet
    pain!

So in this pleasant islet, O no longer will I stay—
And the shadowy summer-dwelling, I will leave this
    very day;
On Arapá I'll launch my skiff and soon be borne away
    From all that feeds this feeling, O this fond sweet
    pain!

I'll go and see dear Rima—she'll welcome me I know,
And a flaxen cloak, her gayest, o'er my weary
    shoulders throw,
With purfle red and points so free—O quite a lovely
    show—
  To charm away this feeling—O this sad sweet pain!

Two feathers I will borrow, and so gracefully I'll wear,
Two feathers soft and snowy for my long black
    lustrous hair;
Of the Albatross's down they'll be—O how charming
    they'll look there—
  All to chase away this feeling—O this fond sweet
    pain!

Then the lads will flock around me with flattering talk
    all day—
And with anxious little pinches sly hints of love
    convey;
And I shall blush with happy pride to hear them . . .
    I daresay . . .
  And quite forget this feeling, O this sad sweet pain!

Alfred Domett.

CII.

At Home.

HIGH in her little rose-clad room
  Niched in the winding stair,
My lady sits and looks abroad
  On the wind's thoroughfare.

The roof is tined with cedar-wood,
  The panels golden pine,
The lattice set with lozenges,
  And hung with crimson fine.

The pear-tree wraps her oriel;
  Musk fills the window-frame;
Her paroquet sits in the ring,
  And twitters out her name.

The circling landscape underneath
  Glows through its misty veil;
The thunder-cloud against the wind
  Beats up, a blackening sail.

The sea, that shone like silver scales,
  Fades, tarnished by its breath;
The shaking poplar turns her face
  As in a wind of death.

Still half the fields return the sun,
  Still laughs the running wheat:
The bird sings on—one sheet of flame!
  And now the thunders meet.

But up within the turret-room
  How still it is, how warm!
Shut, like the water-lily's cup
  That closes in the storm.

A kitten coiled upon the chair,
  A half-wrought broidery,
Books on the wall, and passing dreams—
  Perchance a dream of me!

You hear no knock, no creaking door,
  No foot upon the stair,
But Love has stolen the key of thought,
  Before you know he's there.

                            Anne Glenny Wilson.

CIII.

Rosalind.

ROSALIND has come to town!
  All the street's a meadow,
Balconies are beeches brown
  With a drowsy shadow,
And the long-drawn window-panes
Are the foliage of her lanes.

Rosalind about me brings
  Sunny brooks that quiver
Unto palpitating wings
  Ere they kiss the river,
And her eyes are trusting birds
That do nestle without words.

Rosalind! to me you bear
   Memories of a meeting
When the love-star smote the air
   With a pulse's beating:
Does your Spirit love to pace
In the temple of that place?

Rosalind! be thou the fane
   For my soul's uprising,
Where my heart may reach again
   Thoughts of heaven's devising:
Be the solace self-bestowed
In the shrine of Love's abode!

                  Hubert Church.

CIV.

Of a Lady.

HER house is nearly in the town,
   Yet lilac branches shade her door;
Her tea is always on the board
    At half-past four.

Her fireside has a friendly look:
   There's something happy in the air;
Her cream is such you rarely now
    Meet *any*where.

I like her eyes, I like her hair,
   I like that pretty, simple dress
(Paris, and cost five hundred francs,
    No penny less).

Pardon my inconsiderate words;
  I should not write on themes like these.
(Her shoes are neat; you'd never think
      They're No. 3's).

She likes this shaded corner best,
  The rosy lamp, the Dresden set,
A friend or two, perhaps, a waft
      Of mignonette.

And some one touches in the gloom
  The harp's mysterious, wailing strings,
And thoughts that never spoke in words
      Take music's wings.

Dear friend, though tired and far away,
  I still can seek your door in Spain,
Sit still beside your fire and drink
      That tea again!

  Anne Glenny Wilson.

cv.

Her Secret.

SHE moves sedate, through garden ways
  Or ancient parlours cool and shady;
Content in quiet length of days,
  A typical old maiden lady.
With soul as snowy as the lace
  That lappets o'er her faded tresses,
And sweet as violet's fragrant trace
  That haunts her quaintly fashioned dresses.

One single crime her heart within,
    In quiet hours of meditation
Must be confessed, a hidden sin
    To stir that soul to trepidation.

For when in maiden age one stands
    Left neither soured nor broken-hearted,
Tradition this at least demands!—
    Nor faithful to some long departed:
When midst the records of the years
    One finds no sign to sorrow over;
No yellowing letters stained with tears,
    No least remembrance of a lover!
Hidden in sacredness apart,
    No withering blossoms loved and guarded—
What wonder that the saintliest heart
    Should feel the slightest bit defrauded?

Dear is the ancient maiden dame
    To maiden belles of modern dances;
And girlish fantasies they frame
    Of long-past, ever-fresh romances.
And if they deem such history
    She treasures, safe from rash intrusion—
She would not tell the whitest lie,
    Yet still, she fosters the delusion.
A smile, a sigh, is all they ask
    To furnish hints for fancy's weaving;
She takes her tender soul to task
    For such unparalleled deceiving!

"What changed her fate? and how, and when?"
  "What crossing chanced of love and duty?"
"She scarce was wondrous fair, but then,
  Is every married dame a beauty?"
'Tis strange how brightest maids will love
  A passing woefulness to borrow;
They treasure, happier thoughts above,
  This mystery of secret sorrow.
Their hearts are fluttering to condole
  With grief such tenderest pity moving—
And she a gentle lonely soul,
  That no one ever thought of loving!

Mary Colborne-Veel.

CVI.

The Mother.

My heart is o'erflowing,
  My foot treads the foam,
Go tell to the wide world
  My son has come home
From the far-rolling north sea,
  Where mermaidens cry,
Where the sun, all the week long,
  Goes round in the sky,
Where the ice-cliffs break seaward
  With thunder-loud fall,
From the pale northern dancers—
  He comes from you all!

Go, seek in the oak-chest
   The blue-flowered plate,
The bowl like an eggshell,
   The cup's silver mate.
Lay on the round table
   The damask so fine,
And cut the black cluster
   Still left on the vine.
My hand shakes—but bring me
   That pure honeycomb,
Now nothing shall vex me,
   My boy has come home!

Now twine on the doorway
   Pale wreaths of jasmine,
And tell all the village
   His ship has come in.
How lucky my wheat-bread
   Was baked yester night;
He loves the brown home-loaf,
   And this is so light.
Now heap up wild berries
   As black as the sloe—
I never must tell him
   I've wept for him so!

The girls will come running
   To hear all the news,
The neighbours with nodding
   And scraping of shoes.
The fiddler, the fifer,
   Will play as they run,

The blind beggar, even,
  Will welcome my son.
He smiles like his father
  (I'll sit here and think),
Oh, could he but see us—
  It makes my heart sink.
But what is that?—"Mother!"
  I heard some one call.
"Oh, Ronald, my first-born,
  You've come after all!"

Anne Glenny Wilson.

CVII.

The Bonnie Harvest Moon.

OF all the seasons in the year,
  I like the autumn best,
Ere winter comes with giant strength,
  Or Flora gangs to rest;
When scented breezes fill the air,
  When distant echoes croon,
And ower the hill peeps lazily
  The bonnie harvest moon.

I like to hear the reapers' sang.
  To me 'tis sweeter far
Than a' the sangs that e'er were sung
  In praise of cruel war; . . .
When golden waves sweep o'er the fields,
  When thistles shed their down,
And ower the hill peeps lazily
  The bonnie harvest moon.

John Barr of Craigilee.

CVIII.

Song.

O MERRY be the ploughboy
    That whistles o'er the lea,
And blithesome be the ploughboy
    That comes at e'en to me;
When the bonny moon is shining,
    And the distant echoes fa',
I'll meet my gallant ploughboy,
    The kindest o' them a'.

O merry be the ploughboy
    That whistles through the glen,
When the happy birds are singing,
    In their woodland cozie den;
Where wild flowers sweet are blooming,
    And the scented breezes blaw,
I'll meet my gallant ploughboy,
    The kindest o' them a'.

O merry be the ploughboy
    That whistles in the morn,
When ower the rigs sae gracefully
    He throws the yellow corn.
I winna seek for gowd or gear,
    To make me proud or braw;
My heart is wi' the ploughboy,
    The kindest o' them a'.

John Barr of Craigilee.

CIX.

Morning Invocation.

DEAREST and fairest! sweetest and rarest!
  Arise! come away!
O'er rock and mountain, o'er wood and fountain
  Breaks day.
The mists of the morn from the mountain are rolled:
The dew gleams with gold.

Where ferns are darkling, where rills are sparkling,
  The morning breathes joy.
Waving and looping, the wild flowers are drooping
  And coy:
While echo repeats all the voices of morn,
On quiet winds borne.

Come! for the glory lies varied before thee:
  The blue of the sky
No beauty can render like that which makes tender
  Thine eye:
While spendthrifts in spirit and misers in joy,
Our hours we employ.

H. L. Twisleton.

CX.

My Ain Dearie.

It's ower yonder hill, and it's through yonder glen,
  Whaur the burn rins doun sae clearly,
When the moon shines sae bricht, and the stars gie
    their licht,
  I'll gang then and see my ain dearie.

For she's leal and true, and she's fair to the view,
  Though she be nae a high-born leddy;
She's fair in every part, and she's leddy o' my heart,
  And to mak' her my bride I am ready.

As the rosebud that blaws, and the sna' drift that fa's,
  Is the hue o' her cheek that's sae bonnie;
While the lustre o' her een marks her out for
    beauty's queen,
  And the ploughboy she lo'es best o' ony.

I'll big a wee house in yon cozie den,
  Whaur the wild birds warble sae clearly,
Whaur the kind word and smile shall every care
    beguile,
  And the frowns o' the great winna fear me.

O love is the lowe to licht us through this world,
  Without it the road would be dreary;
Wi' discord, toil, and strife, as the portion o' our life,
  And nae resting-place for the weary.

John Barr of Craigilee.

CXI.

A Roundel.

ONCE in a while the skies seem blue,
    The way grows pleasant for a mile;
Fair blossoms spring where no flowers grew—
        Once in a while.

We leave the road—and mount the stile,
    And hear the throstle's song anew—
An anthem in a vaulted aisle.

Grief loses somewhat of its hue,
    Tired, tear-worn eyes look up and smile,
When God's sweet sunshine stealeth through,
        Once in a while.

W. Francis Chambers.

CXII.

Herdin' the Kye.

THE wild snaw-clouds were driftin'
    Athart the wintry sky,
As thro' the gusty gloamin'
    I went to herd the kye.
I row'd my plaidie roun' me,
    An' shiver'd in the blast;
When o'er the knowe cam' Jamie,
    An' clasp'd me close an' fast!

I saw nae mair the snaw-clouds,
  The sky seem'd bonnie blue,
Refleckit frae my lad's e'en,
  That thrill'd me thro' and thro'.
The nippin' blast nae langer
  Could do me ony skaith,
For luve was in my laddie's clasp
  Eneuch to warm us baith!

Frae aff my lips sae blae-like
  He kiss'd the cauld awa,
I' faith, that bleak gray hillside
  Seem'd sunny to us twa!
Why, then, should Winter fash me,
  Hail, rain, an' snaw thegither?
As lang 's my laddie lo'es me,
  "Twill aye be Simmer weather!

Marie R. Randle.

CXIII.

O Day of Happiness.

O DAY of happiness! O blissful hour!
  She comes across the fields whom all men bless.
Behind her buds of gladness spring and flower,
  O day of happiness!
  Lightly she moves, and hardly seems to press
The solid earth, yet with her joy and power
  Flow free to lift the lowly in distress.

And she is mine: she leaves her maiden bower
  For me, O wonder! Little winds caress
And kiss her curling hair; O blissful hour,
  O day of happiness!

Mary E. Richmond.

CXIV.

Consummation.

THE perfect night is here; each shining star
  Beams at its brightest, and the rolling sphere
Is full of dim enchantments from afar:
  The perfect night is here!
  O Lord of Love and Life! in holy fear
I kneel and pray, no dissonance may mar
  The marriage of our spirits; draw Thou near,
Thou knowest, Father, what Thy children are;
  Make Thou this day of marvels yet more dear;
For now, soft curtained in her glancing car,
  The perfect night is here.

Mary E. Richmond.

CXV.

Enlightenment.

A WOMAN, ere Love gives her light,
  Is sweetly cold, and like a rose,
Whose unblown petals, pure and white
  Its rarest essences enclose;
So chaste and still and sealed from sight,
  Her spirit in its maiden-snows.
But when she knows! Ah! when she knows!

H

And reads Love's miracle aright,
'Tis like the opening of the rose,
'Tis like the melting of the snows,
A flower unfolding to the light,
Petal by petal, to disclose
A spirit delicate and bright,
She blooms and quickens in Love's sight,
And at her heart appearing, shows
A seed of flame, a living light
That fires each petal thro', and grows,
Till like a flame her spirit glows,
Burning, ineffable, and white.

Isabel Maud Peacocke.

CXVI.

Told by the Sea.

A ROSE-HUED time it was to me—
   A day of happiness so strange.
We stood beside the sapphire sea,
   Behind us was the wooded range

That brooded in the sunset's gold
   O'er faerie lore the warm winds brought;
From many a field and laughing wold,
   Where men and women lived and wrought.

The warm wind's breath soon hushed to rest,
   And salt sea-scents spread far and wide.
A white bird called from out the west
   Whence purpling shadows came to bide,

And softly steal round stock and stone
  With deftest touch enfolding all,
While still the low sweet undertone
  From sea-caves seemed to rise and fall.

And gold the strand on which we stood,
  That perfect eve beside the sea,
And talked of much so new and good,
  And forged for problems deep a key.

But when we turned us to depart
  I lingering looked on sky and sea,
To take that picture to my heart.
  You waited too—then reverently

You took my heart within your palm,
  And softly turned the leaves and read,
And then you turned the cover down,
  "I love you, love!" you gently said,

And crowned me queen straightway, O king!
  Wherefore my feet for evermore
Go softly, and the air's a-ring
  With music sweet—unheard before.

                    Dolce A. Cabot.

The Forest City.
(*To Egeria.*)

THERE is a City where the full pulse beats
  Of gentle Nature; parks about it close
  Lit with wind-walking trees in laughing rows,
There, fresh and cool, the wood walks in the streets
Wide-armed, to soothe life's fervours and defeats,
  There, o'er the mart the dew-drenched garden grows,
  And, winding through, a willowed river flows
Rich with clear shades and luminous retreats.

So too, parks close about this heart of mine
  Planted with thoughts of you, and they intrude
  Upon its barren ways, a multitude
Of rustling joys, of presences divine;
  The stream called Happy Love beside them runs
  To mirror them, with God's eternal suns.

W. H. Joyce.

A Folk Song.

I CAME to your town, my love,
  And you were away, away!
I said "She is with the Queen's maidens;
  They tarry long at their play.
They are stringing her words like pearls
To throw to the dukes and earls."
    But O the pity!
I had but a morn of windy red
To come to the town where you were bred,
  And you were away, away!

I came to your town, my love,
　And you were away, away!
I said, "She is with the mountain elves
　And misty and fair as they.
They are spinning a diamond net
To cover her curls of jet."
　　But O the pity!
I had but a noon of searing heat
To come to your town, my love, my sweet,
　And you were away, away!

I came to your town, my love,
　And you were away, away!
I said "She is with the pale white saints,
　And they tarry long to pray.
They give her a white lily crown,
And I fear she will never come down."
　　But O the pity!
I had but an even gray and wan
To come to your town and plead as man,
　And you were away, away!

　　　　　　　　　　Jessie Mackay.

CXIX.

A Vigil.

ONE bird upon the roof,
　A chorister forlorn,
　　Sings to the cloistered morn
Hid in her cloudy woof
　A song that doth unfold
　　Itself in plaited gold.

Sing what I ne'er can say—
  The wave may love the shore,
  The flowers the dews that pour,
The tired winds love to stay
  On cliffs where moss has lain,
  Spent with the toiling main. . . .

Dearer to me one heart
  Where I would love to dwell,
  Woven with magic spell
Into its inner part,
  Sunk in its secrecy
  Like a star in the sea.

Hubert Church.

CXX.

My Song.

I BADE my love Good-night,
  So loth to part
With her, the deep delight
  Of this true heart,
  My queen of pearls!
  My lily of girls!
And when her light was low,
  And all was still,
Saving that rapturous flow—
  The lone bird's trill,

I said:
"Oh, come fair dreams
To soothe her pretty head;
Float soft as silvery beams
Now shed!"
Then up where the lattice swung,
I sent a kiss,
In the heart of a rose there flung,
And murmured this:
"Good-night, Sweet!
Sweet, good-night!
My heart's delight,
Good-night!"

I bade my love Good-morn,
With joy to feel
Her presence, soft as dawn,
Within me steal,
My queen of pearls!
My lily of girls!
And when she came to me
On tiny feet,
I vowed there ne'er could be
A maid so sweet!
Her hair—
The golden sun,
Her cheeks—the rose-bloom rare;
Was ever beauty won
So fair?
The love-light in her eyes
Drew forth my kiss;

I clasped her to me—mine! My prize!
   The greeting this:
   "Good-morn, Sweet!
   Sweet, good-morn!
   My heart's pure dawn,
      Good-morn!"

Charles Umbers.

CXXI.

Cradle Song.

Song of the night, song of the day,
Where are the forms that we fondled alway?
Song of the eve, song of the morn,
Soon they forsake us as others are born;
Mothers sit watching with faces of love,
God watches them from His Heaven above;
Life is a task, set with a vow,—
Babies that slept in us, where are ye now?

Up from our arm, up from our breast,
Where are ye wandered in East or in West?
Mothers may love, mothers may croon,
Ye become stripling and maiden too soon;
Stripling and maiden,—and lo the refrain
Crooned by the mother is murmured again:
Life is a war, life is a race,—
Over the cradle a heavenly face.

"Son of my heart, where wilt thou go?
Empty mine arms when thou leavest me so;—
Where wilt thou speed, daughter of mine?
Look in my face as I looked upon thine;—
Earth is a wilderness open and wide;
Shun ye its evil, and God be your Guide:
Children of mine, go on your way—
Think ye of mother when ageing and grey!

"Goest so soon, idol of love?
Goest so soon to the Father above?
Thou in mine arms cradled shalt be;—
Goest so soon from thy cradle and me?
Earth is too wide for thy weak little feet?
Life is too weary?—and Heaven so sweet?
Idol of love; soul of my heart;
Heaven is thine who of Heaven wast part."

Life and its toil, death and its sleep,
Children must wander and mothers will weep;
Life is so wide, death is so cold,
Other embraces than mother's enfold:—
Children are mothers and mothers are gone,
Cradles are rocking for evermore on;
Children are born, never remain,—
Life is a rocking of pleasure and pain.

Johannes C. Andersen.

CXXII.

Slumber Song.

Now the golden day is ending,
See the quiet night descending,
Stealing, stealing all the colours, all the roses from the
west.
Safe at home each bird is keeping
Watch o'er nest and children sleeping,
Dreaming tender dreams of sunshine, sleeping warm,
for sleep is best.
Sleep then, sleep, my little daughter,
Sleep to sound of running water,
Singing, singing through the twilight, singing little
things to rest.

Down beside the river flowing,
Where the broom and flax are growing,
Little breezes whisper gently, as night's music softly
swells;
And like bells of Elfin pealing,
Lonely through the shadows stealing,
Tinkling, tinkling through the twilight comes the
sound of cattle bells.
Sleep, then, sleep, my little daughter,
Cattle bells, and wind, and water,
Weaving, weaving chains of slumber, cast about thee
Dreamland's spells.

Mary H. Poynter.

CXXIII.

Lullaby.

DAY has fled to the west afar,
Where no shadows or sorrows are;
O'er earth's radiant western rim
God has gathered the day to him.
Hush! the river of night is here,
Flowing silently, cool and clear,
With its mystical thoughts that throng
And its silences deep as song.

> *Babe of my bosom, sleep;*
> *Tender, sweet blossom, sleep!*
>   *Hearts may ache*
> *While the long hours go creeping;*
>   *Hearts may break*
> *While my baby is sleeping;*
>   *Never wake,*
> *Though thy mother is weeping;*
>   *Babe of my bosom, sleep!*

Sleep! the silence is all around,
Save the sighings that are not sound,
Where the wind in the branches weaves
Mystic melodies through the leaves;
Or the far-away murmurings
Like the stir of an angel's wings.
Only night is about us now—
Child, the earth is as tired as thou.

Babe of my bosom, sleep;
Tender, sweet blossom, sleep!
  Hearts may ache
While the long hours go creeping,
  Hearts may break
While my baby is sleeping;
  Never wake,
Though thy mother is weeping;
  Babe of my bosom, sleep!

Arthur H. Adams.

CXXIV.

Slumber Song.

NEITHER to fight nor plead, my dear!
  Home to the low long nest
On the holy sod of the plains of God!
  And it's only to rest, to rest!

Neither to sift nor weigh, my dear!
  Neither to sow nor reap!
For the balance is true and the sickle is through,
  And it's only to sleep, to sleep!

Neither to will nor plan, my dear!
  Neither to smile nor sigh;
For home is the fruit to the altar-foot,
  And it's only to die, to die!

Jessie Mackay.

CXXV.

"If One Rose Should Creep."

IF one rose should creep
　　To bow herself upon the grass
Where Thou art buried (ah, too deep!)
　　And tremble when the angels pass,
She could not reach Thee, Dear, asleep.

But my heart shall wind
　　About Thee in this secret place,
To leave all shadows far behind,
　　And gather all thy sweetness, Grace,
Into the chambers of the mind.

Hubert Church.

CXXVI.

Love's Treasure-house.

I WENT to Love's old Treasure-house last night,
Through soundless halls of the great Tower of Time,
And saw the miser Memory, grown grey
With years of jealous counting of his gems,
At his old task within the solitude.
By a faint taper the deep-furrowed face,
Heavy with power, lay shadowed on the wall—
Shadow and shadowy face communing there—
While the lean flame a living spear-point leaped
With menace at the night's dark countenance.

"And this," he said, "is gold from out her hair,
And this the moonlight that she wandered in,
With here a rose, enamelled by her breath,
That bloomed in glory 'tween her breasts, and here
The brimming sun-cup that she quaffed at noon,
And here the star that cheered her in the night;
In this great chest, see curiously wrought,
Are purest of Love's gems." A ruby key,
Enclasped upon a golden ring, he took,
With care, from out some secret hiding-place,
And delicately touched the lock, whereat
I staggered, blinded by the light of things
More luminous than stars, and questioned thus—
"What are these treasures, miser Memory?"
And slowly bending his grey head, he spoke:
"These are the multitude of kisses sweet
Love gave so gladly, and I treasure here."

D. M. Ross.

CXXVII.

A Dirge.

COME not with sundered flowers to strew her grave;
Nor be there any curtain but the grass,
Dewed by the Night and by the winds that pass
Tranced with the slumber of the level wave;
Or if one cloud of the empyrean nave
Shall float a shadow on her shrouded face,
Be it the shrine of this mysterious place,
Bestowing shelter she for ever gave:

And if the anthem of this holy rood
Fall from the throat of some forgotten bird,
Faint with the press of heaven upon his wings,
Be it the bruised fragrance that is stirred
In the sad heart, remembering happier things
That are the angels of this solitude.

Hubert Church.

CXXVIII.

The Power of Death.

THEY said, "Beneath the iron spell of Death
  The miser recks not for his golden store,
  The craven's heart doth quake with fear no more;
The warrior sleeps, while war drum thundereth;
The patriot, too, 'mid Freedom's glorious strife,
  The wanderer yearns not for his native heath,
  The poet thrills not at Spring's magic breath."
But passively I heard. I thought of Life.

But when they said, "Should, haply, Death thee slay
  And she who is the star of thy Life's night
  Should come and call thy name, thou wouldst not
      heed;"
Then rushed on me like night on tropic day
The consciousness of all Death's awful might.
  I moaned, "O Death, thou potent art, indeed."

C. J. O'Regan.

CXXIX.

Pax Vobiscum.

In a forest, far away,
One small creeklet, day by day,
Murmurs only this sad lay:
   "Peace be with thee, Lilian."

One old box-tree bends his head,
One broad wattle shades her bed,
One lone magpie mourns the dead:
   "Peace be with thee, Lilian."

Echoes come on every breeze,
Sighing through the ancient trees,
Whisp'ring in their melodies:
   "Peace be with thee, Lilian."

Mellow sunbeams, morn and eve,
Quick to come and slow to leave,
Kiss the quilt where daisies weave
   Rich designs o'er Lilian.

When the dying blossoms cling
To the skirts of parting Spring,
Wattle-boughs and branches fling
   Showers of gold o'er Lilian.

When the summer moon mounts high,
Queen of all the speckless sky,
Shafts of silver softly lie
   O'er the grave of Lilian.

Mystic midnight voices melt
Through each leafy bower and belt,
Round the spot where friends have knelt—
  "Peace be with thee, Lilian."

Far away from town and tower,
Sleeping in a leafy bower,
Withered lies the forest flower—
  "Peace be with thee, Lilian."

There, where passions ne'er intrude,
There where Nature has imbued
With her sweets the solitude,
  Rests the form of Lilian.

Dear old forest o'er the sea,
Home of Nature's euphony,
Pour thy requiem psalmody
  O'er the grave of Lilian.

Guard that daisy-quilted sod:
Thou hast there no common clod;
Keep her ashes safe; for God
  Makes but few like Lilian.

Sceptics ask me: "Is that clay
In the forest far away
Part of her?"—I only say:
  "Flow'rets breathe out Lilian;

"From her grave their sweets mount high—
Love and beauty never die—
Sun and stars, earth, sea and sky
  All partake of Lilian."

                  Thomas Bracken.

CXXX.

At Evening.

To break the stillness of the hour
　　There is no sound, no voice, no stir;
　　Only the croak of frogs,—the whirr
Of crickets hidden in leaf and flower.

The clear-cut outlines of a spire
　　Spring from a mass of eucalypt
　　Sharply against the sky,—still tipped
With one last gleam of lingering fire.

So solemnly the shadows creep;
　　On dovelike wings Night flutters down;
　　Lights twinkle in the little town;
The valley lies in quiet sleep.

So comes the dark, so fades the light,
　　On all those leagues of tossing sea
　　That lie between my home and me,
And glimmer to the stars all night.

And so, belovëd, silently
　　In thine own land the shadows fall
　　On grassy lawn, and garden-wall,
On shining sand, and troubled sea,—

On paths thy feet shall never tread,—
　　On fields thine eyes shall never see,—
　　And on thy new home, strange to me,
That silent City of the Dead!

Yea, stillness rests, O Tried and True,
  On hand and heart, on lips and eyes!
  On thee eternal silence lies,
On thee is utter darkness too.

We lost too much in losing thee,
  Yet we who knew and loved thee best,
  Wish thee an everlasting rest,
Night came on thee so quietly.

Peace with the Shadows! Peace to all
  Who work and weep, who pray and wait;
  Till we and thou are one with Fate,
And on us too, the Night shall fall!

Dora Wilcox

CXXXI.

To One Who Loved Me.

O MY lost Love! Where are Thou now?
Still in the flesh, I know, for how
Could thy Soul pass from Earth and I
Not know it? But beneath what sky
Dost Thou in joyous freedom roam,
What happy country is Thy home?
Who bless the Heaven that sent Thee to
Their coasts, a Revelation new
Of Goodness—that is God—of Beauty,
And Love, the fountain-head of Duty,
His other titles? Who doth press
Thine hand and drink the tenderness

Of Thine eye-beams, and raptured hear
Those lips breathe musically clear,
Witchingly soft? Who strokes the fair
Brown ripples of Thy streaming hair,
And feels he dareth overmuch—
For there is magic in its touch?

O Love! Where'er the waves have tost
The pearl of price that I have lost;
Heaven grant some merchant, skilled to tell
The worth hid in the precious shell
May find Thee, sell his all, and be
Content to live and die for Thee!

David Will M. Burn.

CXXXII.

Liebesweh.

Ah, my heart, the storm and sadness!
  Wind that moans, uncomforted,
  Requiem for Love that's dead,
      Love that's dead!
  Leafless trees that sough and sigh,
  Gloom of earth, and grey of sky,
Ah, my heart, what storm and sadness!

Ah, my heart, those sweet Septembers!
  Ah, the glory and the glow
  Of the Spring-tides long ago,
      Long ago!
  Gleam of gold, and glint of green
  On the grassy hillsides seen,
Ah, my heart, those sweet Septembers!

Ah, my heart, on sweet soft pinions,
  Spring, the lov'd one, hovers nigh,
  She shall settle by-and-by,
      By-and-by!
  But the hills shall shine in vain,
  Love, alas, comes not again,
Ah, my heart, on sweet soft pinions!

Dora Wilcox.

CXXXIII.

The Saddest Cross.

He who hath walked in darkness since his birth,
  Who ne'er hath known the glory of the day,
Alike to him are shadow and sun-ray;
  He never wearies at the daylight's dearth.
But he who once hath revelled in Life's mirth
  Right heartfully, and now must ever stray
Where sunbeams never either laugh or play,
  He bears the saddest cross in all the earth.

Lord, long content I wandered in the night:
  Knowing not light, the dark seemed good to me,
Then didst Thou curse me with divinest sight,
  A space I looked on Love's divinity.
Ah, God, if I had never known that light,
  I ne'er had known how dark these shadows be.

C. J. O'Regan.

Song.

ONE eve I saw the hills all flushed with light,
And burnished with the gold of sunset glow—
  The flaming gold of sunset glow.

Next morn, when I arose, the hills were white,
All gleaming cold, and white with early snow;
  And lowering skies above the snow.

One day I plucked a rose that pleased my sight;
But in my garden now no roses blow—
  No more for me red roses blow!

So was my joyous youth gone in a night,
And Love!—Love left me, ah! so long ago
  I scarce remember it—so long ago!

Maud Goodenough Hayter.

Ideal Beauty.

ABSOLVE me for a while, undo
  The links that bind me as your thrall.
So I be more myself, more worthy you;
Let me forget you too in dreams,
  Your lang'rous waist and musical
Soft ways, like cadences of streams
  Unlooked for, strange, but sweetly rhythmical;

The morning freshness of the rose,
  The suave, strong motion of the sea,
The strenuous splendour and repose
  Of marble, and the lily's purity;

All these are types that symbolize
  The secret charm, the subtle grace,
The music as of Paradise
  That plays about your lissom limbs and face;

Let me forget all these and be
  Once more self-centred, circumspect,
And of dædalian longings free.
  Let me a fuller, stronger life elect;

So may I on a windy shore
  See screaming seagulls flying near,
And hear the hollow channels roar,
  Nor seek in every breeze your voice to hear:

Or where the glints of sunshine steal
  Through clust'ring clematis and fern,
There let me roam alone and feel
  The simple joys of sense for which I yearn;

The lights and shadows of the bush,
  The prattling music of the creek,
The stir of insects, and the hush
  Of Solitude—these are the joys I seek.

Oh idle words! Since Marsyas died,
  How many has Apollo slain?
And ah! how many too have tried
  To win you or to shun you—but in vain.
                                  Ebenezer Storry Hay.

Faerie.

WHY have we in these isles no fairy dell,
No haunted wood, nor wild enchanted mere?
Our woods are dark, our lakelets' waters clear,
As those of any land where fairies dwell.
In every verdant vale our streamlets tell
Their simple story to the list'ning ear,
Our craggy mountains steep are full of fear,
E'en rugged men have felt their awful spell.

Yet lack they glamour of the fairy tale,
Nor gnome nor goblin do they e'er recall,
Though Nature speaks, e'en in the wind's sad wail.
Who shall give meaning to Her voices all?
The poet's art,—as yet without avail,—
Must weave the story of both great and small.

Alexander Bathgate.

Fairyland.

As we went down to Fairyland
   We plucked the purple heather,
And all its little tinkling bells
   Sang "Happy be together."

As we went down to Fairyland
   We walked through meadows green,
And the little daisies bowed to us,
   And hailed us king and queen.

As we went down to Fairyland
 We heard the sunbeams singing.
"We weave you robes of rainbows bright
 As the love your hearts are bringing."

As we went down to Fairyland
 Men's voices called from far,
"Poor fools, they walk in golden mists,
 Nor know what fools they are!"

Yet we went on to Fairyland
 And found such blissful greeting
We longed to stay for ever there,
 But ah, its joys were fleeting!

And we came out of Fairyland,
 As many have come before;
And the heather-bells and sunbeams sang
 Their songs to us no more.

But as we left sweet Fairyland
 We heard an old man say,
"Though fools may enter Fairyland,
 Only the wise may stay."

Annie Colborne-Veel.

CXXXVIII.

The Elfin Dell.

WHERE the water tumbles,
　　Into shadow turns,
Where the dead tree crumbles
　　Bound about with ferns,
Hark! a sound of distant beating—
　　　Ting! Ting! Ting!
The busy elfin smiths are meeting,
Hidden sunlit forges heating—
　　　Ting! Ting! Ting!
While tuis in the sunlight swing
　　We hear the anvils ring.

Tread you ne'er so lightly,
　　Stand you ne'er so still,
Two bird-eyes watch brightly,
　　A robin from the hill:
That's their watchman;—still you hear them,—
　　　Ting! Ting! Ting!
Fairies clearly!—why then fear them?
But, when now you think you're near them,
　　　Ting! Ting! Ting!
The watchman bird has taken wing,—
　　No more the anvils ring!

First they seem behind you,
　　Then they seem before;
Withes loop round and bind you,
　　Struggling binds you more:
Far and far away as ever—
　　　Ting! Ting! Ting!

Yes, the elfin smiths are clever;
You know they're near, but see them,—never!
    Ting! Ting! Ting!
Beating in a magic ring
    The unseen hammers swing.

  If only once you could be
    With those fairies far:
   They're always where you would be,
    But never where you are!
Perhaps the ferns and flowers they're making;—
    Ting! Ting! Ting!
Soon as day from night is breaking,
Hark! the elfin smiths are waking—
    Ting! Ting! Ting!
Clear as birds that round them sing
    The elfin anvils ring.

Johannes C. Andersen.

CXXXIX.

Embers.

LITTLE men with red caps delving in the embers,
Looking for the lost flame nobody remembers;
Looking for the Yule log, looking for the laughter,
Fearful of the grey ash soon to follow after.

Youth is like the Yule log, middle life the embers,
Age but the ashes of a cycle of Decembers.
Youth is like the Yule log, lit with merry laughter;
Careless of the grey ash soon to follow after.

Tick, tock, tick, tock, still the hours are flying,
Twenty brave pixie men; twenty shovels plying. . . .
Youth is like the Yule log, but middle age remembers
Little men with red caps delving in the embers.

Winifred S. Tennant.

CXL.

The Nixie's Prayer.

THERE'S never a saint on the floor of heaven,
  Never a saint to pray to!
Nor seraph white at the Nixie's need
  To mourn the livelong day to!
For the word that made the good red blood
  And the golden clay of woman
Went by the dew-born Nixie folk
  That wear but the shape of human.

My father was an elfin king
  Where the last world-water stilleth;
My mother was a rosy wraith
  That shared the dule of Lilith.
I was born in a pearly bower
  Between the sea and Eden;
And given the wide forwandered foam
  To nurse my elfin need in.

So it's well-a-way to the waning moon!
  For the wild witch drop that's in her
Cries down the dewy lift to me
  That never was saint or sinner.
Give me a heart, my Lady Moon,
  Be it but a cup for sorrow!
Give me a heart to-night, to-night,
  Though it should break to-morrow!

Give me the wounded breast of Eve,
  To chrisom child a heaven!
Give me the weeping eye of Eve,
  Forgiving and forgiven!
Give me the hope of mourning Eve
  From Eden gate and onward,—
The robe of living light to be,
  And the throne they build her sunward!

There's never a soul in the waning Moon,
  Never a soul to harken!
She is the Nixie of the sky
  Where the founts of heaven darken.
I am the Nixie of the pool;
  And the star-leaved book we read in
Has never a hope for the Nixie folk
  Between the sea and Eden!

                   Jessie Mackay.

Beauty for Ashes.

My love had in a madhouse been, full seven years and
    more,
Till last night at twilight, there she stood within my
    door!
But she that had been lowly, how grand was now
    her grace:
The dark room was bright with the glory from her
    face.

She said, "I stay'd in prison, to pay my full debt;
I stay'd in school to learn so deep as never to forget.
Touch me not! but tell me, the long way back I've
    come,
Oh, is it to a stranger, or my heart's old home?"

"Never an hour of all the days of the seven years,"
    I said,
"That the door has not been wide for you, and a full
    meal spread.
Horror, Rebellion, and Despair have beggar'd me, 'tis
    true,
But my heart's hearth has kept, see, ever ablaze for
    you!"

"Why, is it seven years," she said, "or seconds, that
    you mean?
Long, long, long, and yet how little it has been!
Seventy years would be little, to have learn'd what
    now I know,
And I'll teach you, Beloved, when I've gone where
    now I go!

"But give me a coal of love," she said, "to warm me
    on my way,
And a little bite and sup of love, to stay me on till
    Day.
Fire and food I'll send you down, when I am safe
    above,
And you'll find then, Beloved, that I've sent you Love
    for love!"

She put her lips to my heart, and kiss'd away the
    seven years' pain;
Cold little hands she put to it, and lo! 'twas warm
    again.
Like a star, a star, she shone . . . across the sill, the
    sod . . .
Till the stars above told me the way she'd gone to
    God.

B. E. Baughan.

CXLII.

Art and Beauty.

I SAW as in a dream a palace high,
   With deep-domed roof on massive columns set,
   Wherein were forms, the loveliest Art had yet
Conceived, which none could over-magnify.
The dome was as a star-bespangled sky,
   The columns richly chased; and there was met
   In every niche a lovely statuette,
And all around Art's glories charmed the eye;

And while I gazed, and thought that here I saw
Man's fairest dreams preserved beyond decay
    The palace fell; and I was filled with awe.
Then lo! there broke the splendours of the day,
    And all things seemed to say in earth and sky,
    "Though Art be mortal, Beauty cannot die."

Henry Allison.

CXLIII.

The Devotee of Art.

Ask me not why I work with so much zeal
    To form the thing that seems to me so fair,
    When over all, in spite of every care,
The lines of slow decay will surely steal.
I work because I must, because I feel
    The sway of Art, its inspiration rare,
    Which leadeth by a broad and lofty stair
To where Truth doth to me herself reveal
    In regal splendour. This I strive to show
That all who see may render homage due.
    For, though my work shall fade, yet well I know,
    If men her beauty see, it shall not die:
In every age they will her face renew,
    And keep her radiant glories ever nigh.

Henry Allison.

CXLIV.

The Quest of the Sancgreal.

WHO seeks the Holy Grail he rides aloof.
  The lure of lips and eyes and rippled hair
  And clinging arms,—all love's white silken snare
He shall thrust from him for his soul's behoof;
And when Night cowers upon Comfort's roof,
  The leaping fire and circling wine forswear,
  And follow where Adventure's clarions blare
And spirit frets its fleshly warp and woof.

The salt of life shall mock with appetite,
  His lips denied the savour and the spice
Wherein the sons of men do take delight;
  He shall enthrone his soul beyond their price,
And follow the cold twilight of the trail,
And in the end he shall not win the Grail.

                    Seaforth Mackenzie.

CXLV.

Quot Oculi Tot Mundi.

THE world is as the sense that makes it known:
  To eyeless creatures, dark eternally;
  To others, dim, in mazy depths of sea,
Beyond the sound of all its surface moan;
Narrow to some, as insects 'neath a stone,
  Or in a tiny crevice, or a bee
  That murmurs in a flower; but the free,
Heav'n-soaring birds a wider vision own.

I

And though our eyes can boast no eagle sweep,
  To us is given the larger range of thought,
Wherewith we pierce the starry depths, o'erleap
  The bounds of sense, and see in all things wrought
Signs of deep mysteries, which angel eyes
May see, or ours, perchance, in paradise.

Henry Allison.

CXLVI.

Prometheus and Asia.

WHEN a rose in beauty blows,
  When a bud from earth outpeeps,
When a soul another knows
  In love's glassy, dreamy deeps,
Is not then Prometheus wed?
Is not then sweet Asia led
  To the spotless bowers of love?
  And love is Lord all things above.

When a toiler finds some law,
  Thro' all change unchangeable,
And in joy and loving awe
  Sees less dim the Eternal Will,
Is not then Prometheus led
Joyous to the nuptial bed?
  Is not then his Asia's rule
  Gracious, loving, beautiful?

When a poet's frenzied brain
   Catches at some hidden truth,
When is wash'd a crimson stain
   With forgiving tears of ruth,
Is not then Prometheus' bride
Standing glowing by his side?
   Is not then more sweet to him
   Than the song of Seraphim
Her sweet breath and placid eyes?
For **Earth is one** with Paradise.

Ebenezer Storry Hay.

CXLVII.

Immortality.

AT twenty-five I cast my horoscope,
   And saw a future with all good things rife—
   A firm assurance of eternal life
In worlds beyond, and in this world the hope
Of deathless fame.   But now my sun doth slope
   To setting, and the toil of sordid strife,
   The care of food and raiment, child and wife,
Have dimmed and narrowed all my spirit's scope.

Eternal life—a river gulfed in sands!
   Undying fame—a rainbow lost in clouds!
   What hope of immortality remains
But this : " Some soul that loves and understands
   Shall save thee from the darkness that enshrouds ; "
   And this : " Thy blood shall course in others'
     veins ? "

John Liddell Kelly.

CXLVIII.

" My Pipe is Small."

MY pipe is small, but I will labour hard
    That naught but melody shall issue thence ;
    And though the song, tumultuous and intense,
Inspired of passion, is to me debarred,
Yet in some golden moments happy-starred
    Apollo holds me in a sweet suspense,
    Breathless and rapt—and straining every sense,
I hear his lyre, and great is my reward.

And oh ! what joy when song has wed to it
    The clanging choral music of the sea,
Or whirr of birds that in green shadows flit
    With brisk and timid flight from tree to tree !—
When sounds like these find voice in what is writ,
    O happy poet ! how I envy thee !

Ebenezer Storry Hay.

CXLIX.

The Shell

(After Herédia)

How many winters past, in Oceans cold,
    Little bright shell—but who shall ever know ?—
    Did the waves rack thee, in billow and current and
        flow,
Through the green deeps of their abysses rolled ?
Now you are safe, warm on this beach of gold,
    Far from the bitter waves of long ago,
    But not at rest.   For always, heavy and low
In your heart swells the great sea-voice of old.

My soul is desolate, and full of sound :
   For as there mourns in the shell's whorléd core
   The olden chanting of the clamorous seas,
So in my heart's depths, filled with Her memories,
   Aches the dull murmur, unconscious, slow, profound,
   Of those far storms of passion evermore.

                  M. C. Keane.

CL.

Sonnet.

THERE be some songs that, whosoever singeth,
Still fall in measured cadence on the ear ;
And soft and slow their music ever ringeth
Adown the weary waning of the year.
All may not think their strains divinest rapture,
But unto us their faintest echo seems
Like unto those that all our senses capture,
Heard in the fairy realms of sweetest dreams ;
And the spell lies in touch of mem'ry's fingers
That wakes within our hearts some answering note—
A note whose blessed sweetness ever lingers
Like the dear sounds from some rare song-bird's throat ;
A lingering note that, from the past, doth borrow
Something of long-gone joy or half-sweet sorrow.

                Clara Singer Poynter.

To Sir George Grey.

WITHIN a forest stood a grand old tree,
   Whose head above the other plants rose high ;
   He was the forest's first-born.   Sun and sky
Had known him, and had smiled on him ere he
   Had kinsfolk near, or leafy brethren nigh ;
The wild birds brought to him their minstrelsy ;
   The singers knew that when the scene was rude,
He grew and gave a shelter to their race.
   By him the wandering melodists were wooed
To trill and warble in that lonely place ;
   A sanctuary in the solitude
He gave to them.   In him the birds could trace
   The forest's king, and so from hills and plains
   They flew to him, and sang their sweetest strains.

                         Thomas Bracken.

CLII.

The Home Coming.

OUT of the West, sound sleeping,
Heedless now of the change of dawn and sunset,
Dreaming deep of the olden clamour and onset,
   Wrapt in peace and swayed in the passionate swell
      Of hurrying waves high leaping
            To foam farewell.

Home to the hills that mourn him !
With silence set on the lips that laughed and lightened,
Darkness set in the clear grey eyes that brightened,
    When once he swept the strings of the songful days.
        High, high, pale Death has borne him
            By far, dim ways.

        Vain now the trumpets' blaring,
The bright, blithe cheers and shouts of the hearts that
        love him.
Wishful only of peace and the grass above him,
    Out of the dark strange sea he is seeking rest.
        Ended his strong wayfaring—
            Closed his long quest.

        Our days go heavily onward,
The light that lit us of old is no more shining ;
The dark has hidden our path beyond divining ;
    The soul that saw the East where the morning gleams
        Has swept in a long flight sunward
            With all its dreams.

        Far past our utmost knowing !
Tears, or desirous hearts, or the death flag streaming
Vex him not in the deeps of his secret dreaming ;
    Passion he knows no more, nor the face of woe,
        Where poppies of peace are glowing,
            And sweet winds blow.

                                M. C. Keane.

CLIII.

The Wit.

WHILE the dull talk idly streams,
He sits upon the bank and dreams,
Till some careless word that's said
Finds a fellow in his head.—

He with one great bound is borne
From Dent Blanche to Matterhorn ;
And his passage is so fast
Over that abyss so vast,
He has not seen how bluely shines
The deep gulf in his pelt of pines,
Nor heard the waste and watery voice
Wherewith the wind-washed pines rejoice.

In a moment's thousandth part,
In the beat of the bee's heart,
He has flown it : 'tis away
Where the kite and eagle play.
Tho' the chamois, lithe and fine,
Passes it 'twixt wake and dine ;
Tho' the dun geier, gaunt and lean,
Flash across that gulf between
Sol's first footing of his bed
And the covering of his head,
What he's compassed in one stride
Is two days for the Zermatt guide.

Arnold Wall.

CLIV.

Fleet Street.

BENEATH this narrow, jostling street,
Unruffled by the noise of feet,
Like a slow organ-note I hear
The pulses of the great world beat.

Unseen beneath the city's show
Through this aorta ever flow
The currents of the universe—
A thousand pulses throbbing low !

Unheard beneath the pavement's din
Unknown magicians sit within
Dim caves, and weave life into words
On patient looms that spin and spin.

There, uninspired, yet with the dower
Of mightier mechanic power,
Some bent, obscure Euripides
Builds the loud drama of the hour !

There, from the gaping presses hurled,
A thousand voices, passion-whirled,
With throats of steel vociferate
The incessant story of the world !

So through this artery from age
To age the tides of passion rage,
The swift historians of each day
Flinging a world upon a page !

And then I pause and gaze my fill
Where cataracts of traffic spill
Their foam into the Circus.   Lo !
Look up, the crown on Ludgate Hill !

Remote from all the city's moods,
In high, untroubled solitudes,
Like an old Buddha swathed in dream,
St. Paul's above the city broods !

Arthur H. Adams.

CLV.

Sonnet on Keats.

Now, while the air is sweet with breath of spring,
  And loud with liquid melody and mirth ;
  When budding flowers burst into early birth,
And orchard trees are white with blossoming,
And on their snowy twigs the sweet birds sing ;
  When beauty is new-born o'er all the earth,
  And with the last chill wind the fear of dearth,
And other piercing fears, have taken wing ;
This is the season I would think of one—
  The dear Endymion, the star-eyed youth—
Who loved the quickened earth as doth the sun,
  Whose heart was full of courage and of ruth,
Whose voice in sweetest melodies would run ;
  And, lo, how Beauty was with him the Truth !

Ebenezer Storry Hay.

CLVI.

Licence.

MUCH is forgiven to a soul in earnest,
Nor shall we carp at clicking heels on the rail,
When a bold leaper leaps his utmost height
With thundery rush, triumphing ; nor complain
When bold Will Shakespeare or our Meredith,
All quivering with the heat and lust of the chase,
Strains out the thews of language to the bursting,
Sets the shy accent toppling on the verge
Of utmost music, poising perilously
Betwixt the gulfs ; or slants the molten thought
Too generously, and flaws the golden mould ;
For who achieves the impossible shall have grace.

Arnold Wall.

CLVII.

Nausicaa.

I SHOULD he happy—all men tell me so.
To-morrow's sun will see my wedding-day,
And all mine handmaids, comrades of my youth,
Cluster around me, babbling of the feast,
Spread in the broad halls of Alcinous,
And never cease to prate of the rich robes
And priceless gems around my chamber hung ;
While my fond mother's face is that of one
To whom the days of far past youth return.
Nay, when my stately father looks on me,
Plays round his firm-set lips a rare, faint smile.

Surely I should be happy, yet, ah yet,
The comely bridegroom whom they chose for me
Stirs not my pulses with his homely speech
And homely manners, by this dull land bred,
Where never yet was heard the clash of arms,
The shout of victory, the warrior's joy.
The too kind Gods have compassed us about
With the broad buckler of the restless sea,
And great Poseidon watches over us,
So that no foeman e'er can work us harm.
In sooth it is not well that men should live
Thus lapp'd in peace through all the countless years.
The very heart of manhood must rot out,
Where none have braved a foe, or dared a wound.
Not always did I think so—these new thoughts
Of manliness and glory broke on me
When first that godlike hero touched our shores,
And told his story, five long years agone.
Let me recall, though the last time it be,
The first sweet words he uttered at my feet :
:" O Queen, I kneel before thee, whether thou
Be goddess or be mortal ; if thou be
A goddess—one of them that hold broad Heaven—
To Artemis, the daughter of great Zeus,
For beauty and for stature and for grace,
Fain would I liken thee ; but if thou be
A child of men who dwell upon this earth,
Thrice blessed are thy sire and sainted mother—
Thrice blessed are thy brethren ; yea their souls
Must burn with gladness for the love of thee
When they behold thee, flower of maidenhood,
Leading the dance.   Beyond all others blest
Is he who woos and wins thee for his home.

For never yet mine eyes have seen thy peer,
Or man or maid ; it awes me to look on thee.
In Delos once I saw a thing as fair—
A palm-shoot springing by Apollo's altar.
(For thither went I, and much people with me ;
Sore woe in time to come that journey wrought me.)
When I long time had gazed thereon, I marvelled,
For never yet from earth rose stem so fair.
So lady do I marvel at thee, and much dread
To touch thy knees, though grief weighs sorely on me.
But yesterday, the twentieth day, I 'scaped
The darkling sea ; till then the wave still bore me,
And fierce blasts drove me from Ogygia's isle.
And here some God hath cast me, that perchance
Still further evil I may yet endure ;
For trow I that not yet my woes will cease,
But many more the Gods have still in store.
Then, queen, have mercy on me ; unto thee
First, after many sufferings, have I come ;
None other do I know of those who hold
This city and this land.   Show me the town,
And if some wrap thou didst bring for thy linen,
Give it me for a garment to cast round me :
So may the Gods grant thee thy heart's desire—
A husband and a home—a mind be thine
At one with his, for nought can better be
Or nobler than when wife and husband keep
Their household with one single heart and mind."
These were the words the kneeling outcast spake.
But though his limbs were all befouled with slime,
And his thick locks were clotted o'er with brine,
His native nobleness shone out through all.
We pitied him.   Who would not pity him ?

Meat, drink and raiment, these my maidens gave ;
The pure stream washed away the rude sea's stains,
While all my handmaids marvelled at the grace
And beauty of this poor waif of the deep.
Then greatly moved, I earnestly bespake them,
" Not without will of all the Gods who hold
Olympus, to Phæacia came this man,
For, whereas erst he seemed uncomely, now
Like to the Gods who hold broad Heaven is he ;
May such be called my husband, dwelling here,
Where it may please him to abide with me."—
Not in our time that day shall be forgot
When—a poor suppliant in my father's halls—
The tale of Troy our blind old minstrel sang
Wrung from the stranger no unmanly tears.
Erect he stood, and flung aside disguise,
Confest a hero and born king of men.
Then, day by day, fell from his honeyed lips
The wondrous story of his full, brave life,
While, spell-bound, all our dull Phæacian youth,
And my dull bridegroom with them, stood agape.
Then came the bitter time, so long delayed,
When from our noble guest we needs must part ;
Few were my farewell words, and his as few.
Before the portal of my father's house
I stood and said, " Farewell !   And think of me
When thou returnest to thy native land,
As of one unto whom thy life thou owest."
Then, as one deeply stirred, these words he breathed :
" Nausicaa, should Zeus and Here grant
That I once more should see my island home,
Daily as to a Goddess, will I pay
My vows to thee, for thou, girl, gav'st me life."—

Did the man love me then ?   Ah me !   I know not.
It were unworthy of a great king's child,
Yes ! most unworthy of a modest maid,
To show my liking for a parting guest ;
Phæacia's daughters are not wont to woo.
So, without further speech, he sailed away.
But yet, at times, I think the stranger loved me,
And, all those years, no day has glided by
But I have seaward cast my longing eyes,
If I might o'er the waves perchance descry
His white sails swollen by the eastern breeze.
In all these years no tidings yet have sped
From the broad outer world to this lone isle,
Girt by the main as by an iron band.
And day by day my home-bred suitor came,
Wooing me with his rough Phæacian speech,
Not like that other's whose clear accents fell
As the smooth rippling of a full-fed stream.
And, as I still delayed, my handmaids said,
" The youth is comely, princess why delay ? "
And my grey mother spake in mild rebuke,
" Daughter, why let the glory of thy youth
Slip idly by ?   Long hath the patient youth
Stood by, expectant ; make him happy now."
Then last of all, my sire, in weighty words,
Told me it was not well a girl of his
Should lack a guardian when her sire was gone,
For his own thread of life was nearly spun—
And so at last I yielded.   Well I wist
That other one would come back nevermore,
And that I had but fed me on a dream.

William Hodgson.

Pan.

Down a west-sloping valley, by a pool
O'er-gilded by the dying summer day,
Piping alone among the sighing reeds,
Mourning for Syrinx by the water-side,
Sat Pan, alone ; soft on the evening breeze,
His low-blown music fluted down the vale.
The trees, the rocks, all Nature heard the sound,
And guessed the words he dare not speak aloud.

" O, cruel nymph, why didst thou flee from me,
Who loved thee with the love thou didst not know,
Who love thee still, though thou art gone from me ?
Long did I seek thee through the dark, sweet shades
Where hidden violets in this ancient wood,
With sweet, fresh fragrance fill the dewy air,
Till, last, I found thee in the mournful reeds
That shiver coldly round this woodland pool.
And now I sit alone among those reeds,
And think of thee departed."

Here the strains
Ceased, and the last notes floated down the vale
Towards the pale-green west, and fresher blew,
Athwart the fragrance of that ancient wood,
The evening breeze, and stirred the hollow reeds,
Making a rustling whisper through the air—
Lost Syrinx's voice—" I prayed unto the Gods
To save me, and they saved me " and again

" Farewell." At this uprose the woodland god
And passed away among the shadowy glades
Down to the western plain. And the pale light
Died in the west, and night fell on the pool.

Tremayne M. Curnow.

CLIX.

The Hosts of Sleep.

OUT of a gold and purple dreamland streaming,
The dark-eyed troops of sleep come swift and silent,
Fling from their thin hands drowsy influences,
          Marching to take
The battled burg of Freewill.

The unleashed thoughts run gamesome in the country,
Each racing other, playing, singing, dancing ;
Some feebly tilling tangled plots of woodland,
          Dark, remote,
Far out from the city.

Some work so hard, and others play so madly,
They do not hear the rustle and the whisper
Of the dark forces thronging out of dreamland,
          Silent, swift,
Breathing scouts before them.

Some are taken, flooded by the vast wave—
Half-thought thoughts, forgotten in the morning,
Workers or players, singers blythe and dancers,
          Prone, cold,
Motionless for ever.

Some catch a distant warning of the army,
And flee swiftly, scurry to the city ;
Safe till to-morrow, safe within the ramparts ;
        Loud, shrill,
The clarions bawl the warning.

The gates are closed, Freewill stands erect, firm ;
Back to the dimly-wooded far horizon
Ebb the dark masses, melting into distance ;
        Back, back,
Streams the host of darkness.

The sentries doze, careless run the young thoughts,
Out again, out, to the empty country,
Panting in their play, in their mazy dances,
        Light, free,
Far from sleep and silence.

Full five times the great host streams up silent,
Laps up the young thoughts, buries them in darkness ;
But the alarm twists upward from the fortress,
        Lank, shrill,
Before they reach the ramparts.

Then all the sentries, weary with long watching,
Hug the propt spear, blink and nod and murmur,
And the last thought, swiftly racing homeward,
        Trips, falls,
Close beside the drawbridge.

Silently and grimly stalk the troops of dreamland ;
There is no alarm ; they swarm upon the high walls,
Take the hushed city, brood upon it darkly,
        Down, down,
Sinks the flag of Freewill.

They hang, like crape before the face of mourners,
Blurring, dimming the features of the city,
The burghers, kingless, they lead in dance fantastic,
　　　　Sleep, armed sleep,
Holds the walls till morning.

Arnold Wall.

CLX.

The Land of My Desire.

A WILD sea-rover, lined and gray,
　　To me long since a story told,
Of meadows far and far away
　　That blossom into flowers of gold ;

Of streams that were long lullabies
　　For ever flowing thro' the vales,
Kissed by a low and loving wind
　　To music like the Nightingale's.

And I who listened, felt the spell
　　Take hold of manhood on its throne,
And, careless then of Heaven or Hell,
　　Took ship unto the vast Unknown.

The morning set the sails afire
　　With flames that kindled all my blood,
As to the Land of my Desire
　　I steered across a foaming flood.

Day after day the Sun did turn
　　From East to West, from sea to sea,
Night after night the Stars did burn
　　Above the Ocean's minstrelsy.

And like a far mirage I seemed
  To see fair woman-faces shine
Where the great moon-washed spaces gleamed
  On league and rolling league of brine.

At times a wayward kiss I quaffed
  From some sea-nymph beside my barque,
But as in very joy I laughed
  The Stars forsook me, in the dark.

One day on the horizon spread,
  Like some long cloud surprised in sleep,
I saw an Island lift its head
  A little way above the deep.

And there, in the cool shadow-time
  I landed, weary of the Sea,
While maidens of the sunny clime
  Gave draught on draught of Love to me.

And when I laid me down to rest
  Tired of the dance, the feast and wine,
And full red lips too closely pressed,
  Too often and too hot, on mine ;

One woke me in the night and said—
  " Receive the crown that thou hast won,"
And placing it upon my head
  She called me her " belovëd one."

And there I saw a harlot stand,
  The lustre dead in eyes and hair,
Alone with me upon the land
  Of my Desire, and . . . . my Despair.

D. M. Ross.

CLXI.

Night Island.

ROCKING upon the spectral sea
A shallop swims awaiting me,
   Boat of the Fay ;
Frail is the crescent, hollowed thin ;
Rapt in a dream I sit therein
   And speed away.

Silent the midnight ; light the fleece
Adrift across the moon of peace
   Through sea-air suave ;
In quivering, wrinkled, broken bars,
The trembling silver of the stars
   Floats on the wave.

No foam is cleft beneath the prow,
No tinkling ripple taps the bow,
   No whitening wake
The magic keel of ivory shows,
That swerves not left or right, but knows
   The way to take.

Fast, o'er the foamless, silent sea
The wistful boat skims eagerly
   Till pale shores rise,
A coast whence rings no pilot's hail.
And there, in deeps no seamen sail,
   Night Island lies.

At first, one cloudy dome, but soon
Flecked like the circle of the moon
   With shadowy shapes,
While slender cones, volcanoes steep,
Piercing dark clouds whose masses sleep
   O'er tree-clad capes.

Forth wafted over the dim flood
The odours of the enchanted wood
   Fresh earth-scents bear ;
Flowers of starlight, wizard dews,
Scents of the mould and leaf, confuse
   The clean, salt air.

Is that the echo of the surge
Caught in yon winding, deepening gorge ?
   Is that the voice
Of yonder foam-pale waterfall,
Of whose blown spray the tree-ferns tall
   Drink and rejoice ?

It is no stream's, no surge's wail,
No night-voice of a mountain vale.
   Lo,—swells the chant !
A human strain is in my ears
Of manhood's passion, woman's tears,
   And dreams that haunt.

Dreams of the lost ideal, ruth
For boyhood's faith and gallant truth
   And youth's brave will ;
Then keenest joy, dear hopes and kind
That thrill the heart, glad tears that blind
   Tired eyes,—and still,

Stayed by a spell the magic boat
A bow-shot from the shore must float
   Nor touch the strand,
Though it can feel the ground-swell's might
Lift and collect itself to smite
   The shelving sand.

Bound, as a dreamer bound in sleep,
Held back, held fast upon the deep,
   The skiff must stay.
Lost as a dream at morning's star
The fairy isle, borne swift and far,
   Fades, fades away.

For never living man may reach
Or leap upon Night Island's beach
   Howe'er he long,
Though many a night in voyage vain
He cross the visionary main
   To hear that song.

          William Pember Reeves.

CLXII.

Night Fancies.

OUT on the silent, darkling sea of Night
  She flies, the airy pinnace of my mind ;
She needs no wind to bear her out of sight,
  No chart her path to find.

But, solely captained by a Shape of Thought,
  She drives upon that foamless ocean, blown
By breath of fancy in her round sails caught,
  Unmarked, unhailed, alone—

From sound or sight or seeking holding so
    Until she casts her crystal anchor down,
Within some starry archipelago,
    Below some dream-built town.

There, gently swinging in that softer air,
    She loads her hold with precious bales of Peace—
From shadowy wharves are passed the bundles rare
    Of Calmness-without-cease.

So turning, silent ever, on that tide,
    Swifter than any bird she wings her way,
Back without falter, where she may abide,
    Close-hidden in the bay

Which is my secret Being, safe from storm—
    Puts off her charmèd cargo, which to me
A quietude of spirit is, the form
    Of a high constancy.

J. C. Beaglehole.

CLXIII.

Mutability.

HERE all is change, and life a deep unrest ;
    So say the waves that break upon the shore,
    The shifting sands that drift for evermore,
The ever-moving crowd that seem possessed
Of souls unquiet as the waves, but blest
    With heedlessness of all that lies before,
    For none may know what changes are in store ;
We can but dream them on soft nature's breast.

Yet, 'neath the waves there dwells eternal calm :
   Delve deep the sand, and to the rock it brings :
   The inconstant crowd is voiceful of the soul,
Which liveth alway, an unfading palm,
   Drawing its life from deep, divinest springs
   That shall not fail while stars and systems roll.

Henry Allison.

CLXIV.

The Deepest Yearning.

OUR life is more than meat.   Deep in the Soul
   Springs Godlike, Godward yearning ; ay, and we,
   Though earth-drawn, ever would rise, unstained and
      free,
Above the clouds of sense that hide our goal.
This wondrous frame of things is as a scroll
   Of mystic import, teaching us to see,
   Though vaguely, and through shrouds of mystery,
The working of that power which moves the Whole.
Not Science fair, though sought with purpose true,
   Nor Art, that all her wealth upon us spends,
Can fill the soul.   She can her strength renew
   Only with bread that from on high descends.
She yearns for That to which all things are due—
   The Centre deep to which all Being tends.

Henry Allison.

CLXV.

Life's Vigil.

A MAN kept vigil by a lonely fire,
Inscrutable the night on every side
Hung round.   The ruddy glow now almost died,
Now, fanned by wandering winds, it flickered higher :
The watcher tended it with ceaseless care,
And ever as it waned he crept still higher,
Till, weary and o'er-watched, he 'gan to tire ;
Then slept.   He woke, and day was shining fair.

Even thus a vigil do all mortals keep
Beside the fire of Life, whose fitful ray
Is girt with night wherethro' no eyes may peep ;
We tend its flickering flame as best we may,
Till weary grown we drowse, then fall asleep,
And when we waken up we find 'tis Day.

C. J. O'Regan.

CLXVI.

Blue Magic.

TEMPLE of Twilight on a lonely hilltop
Towers of pale opal leaning on the sky,
Take my soul lying in the blue-black grasses,
Burn it with blue flame, for to-day I die.

Here in the deep'ning drift of many petals,
Here where the shadows pass with noiseless tread
(Blue phantoms stealing down the silent pine-ways)
Tenderly lay me when my life is fled.

Let only young priests bear my withered body,
Eyes filled with wonder 'neath their azure hoods,
Let only maidens dancing in their frailness
Chant the Blue Magic of the sacred woods.

Pass by and leave me to the peace of silence
Here in the forest and the night's dim blue ;
Soon will the incense in the swinging censer
Cast its last flicker on the ghostly dew.

Only the darkness and the burnt-out torches,
Only the blue pall of the lonely sky,
Only the sighing round the shrouded figure,
Only the wraiths of starlight drifting by.

Death, and a sleeping in the long blue grasses.
Into the Twilight Temple, hush ! he passes !

Marna Service.

CLXVII.

To the Soul.

WHEN the unknown shall be known ;
  When the unseen shall be seen ;
    When thou art strong, and loud, and arisen,
    O Soul, within thy prison,
And the old enchantments flown,
  And men's eyes clear and keen,

Till they see beyond the grave,—
  Till they pierce beneath the flesh,—
    Till the weaker at death no longer
    Are fain of the word of the stronger ;—
" Be brave, my brother, be brave ;
  Thy day beginneth afresh ! "

When good is worn of all,
  Deemed priceless as though rare ;
    When evil has lain forsaken,
    Thrown down long since untaken,
Its strength become so small,
  It is not worth men's wear ;

When the body all work has done,
  And the mind all wisdom learnt,
    And found their labour and learning
    But as toil that brings no earning,
In the face of the full fair sun
  But as needless lanterns burnt ;

When thou, O Soul, art found
  Beneath thy lowly guise ;
    When men have proclaimed thee royal,
    And to thee, and none other, loyal,
Have made thy power to abound
  Till all alike are wise.

But this is not yet ; and now
  The god lies bound in us ;
    Still, searching the dusky portal
    Cloven through all things mortal,
His white and prostrate brow
  We may discover thus.

Are we not each a lamp
  Of frail and earthen form,
    Wherein a spark doth shelter
    Beyond the tempest's pelter,
Lightening the chill and damp,
  Swinging through night and storm ?

We know that clouded light
  Is as the light of stars,
    And though the bowl be broken,
    This is our sign and token,
That flame by mutual might
  Shall climb their shining cars.

Frederick Napier Broome.

CLXVIII.

Not Understood.

NOT understood. We move along asunder,
  Our paths grow wider as the seasons creep
Along the years ; we marvel and we wonder
  Why life is life : and then we fall asleep,
          Not understood.

Not understood. We gather false impressions,
  And hug them closer as the years go by,
Till virtues often seem to us transgressions ;
  And thus men rise and fall, and live and die,
          Not understood.

Not understood. Poor souls with stunted vision
  Oft measure giants by their narrow gauge ;
The poisoned shafts of falsehood and derision
  Are oft impelled 'gainst those who mould the age,
          Not understood.

Not understood. The secret springs of action,
  Which lie beneath the surface and the show,
Are disregarded ; with self-satisfaction
  We judge our neighbours, and they often go,
          Not understood.

Not understood.   How trifles often change us !
  The thoughtless sentence or the fancied slight
Destroy long years of friendship and enstrange us,
  And on our souls there falls a freezing blight ;
                Not understood.

Not understood.   How many hearts are aching
  For lack of sympathy !   Ah ! day by day,
How many cheerless, lonely hearts are breaking !
  How many noble spirits pass away
                Not understood.

Oh, God ! that men would see a little clearer,
  Or judge less harshly where they cannot see ;
Oh, God ! that men would draw a little nearer
  To one another, they'd be nearer Thee,
                And understood.

Thomas Bracken.

CLXIX.

The Answer of the Days.

I SOMETIMES turn from these dark days that be
Backward unto the fair days once I knew—
The far, fair days when all the world seemed true,
Ere yet I learned that joy had wings to flee.
" O Days," I cry, " so wonderful and blue,
Come back again ; come back and bring to me
The silent laughter and the vanished glee ;
Come back, dear days, I swear to cherish you ! "

Then back on me with sad, reproachful eye
Each old Day looks, and voices without sound
Come from them : " Mortal, cease that bootless cry ;
We came to you bliss-laden, and we crowned
Your soul with joys ; and after all we found
You blest us not, but smiled to see us die."

C. J. O'Regan.

CLXX.

A Parable of Fiddles.

SEEING we are as viols to His hand,
I know not whether we should hope or fear
That He should smite a music out of us,
As out of Lear, or Goriot, or Satan—
A tangled wisp of music as from bells
Wind-swung and angry, or a comet-blaze
Of hell-hot harmonies grown slowly cool.

All round His workshop we hang, dusty, silent ;
Will it be wild caprice, or deep design,
Shall move His hand toward this brother or that,
Toward you or me ?

        Will He, like fierce old Saul,
Meshed in a toil of cross desires and fears,
Smooth out the ragged discord of His soul
With some sweet elvish moonlight melody,
As of a lost breeze in the elms of Heaven,
Then break His instrument in ape-like fury,
So that we shriek once and are still for ever ?

Or will He, toying with a single string,
While we lie yet half-made, draw out crude trills,
Mad turns and sweeps, and soulless tremolos,
A hideous parody of music sweet,
Then dash us to the floor as all unfit
For airs divine and themes of Paradise ?

Or shall we meekly pray that we may hang
Mellowing, peaceable, voiceless to the end,
Gathering dust upon the workshop wall ?

Arnold Wall.

CLXXI.

In Days of Peace.

THE stalwart troopers rode at ease,
   In scarlet, gold and steel.
Within the park the worker crept
   To eat his scanty meal.
Alas ! the workers' meals have paid
For sword and horse and golden braid.

The glittering troopers charge along
   The crowded city lanes.
No medicine like steel to soothe
   The gnawing hunger-pains !
Oh ! toilers for the Lords of Trade,
These are the gods your hands have made !

Edward Tregear.

CLXXII.

The Yeoman's Song.

I HEARD a little bird singing in the sky,
   And so gaily he did sing ;—
" There are deaths for the low man, the middle, and
     the high,
   By the grace of our lord the King ! "

I heard a little bird singing in the sky :—
   " In the forest lies a fat buck slain ;
There's a rebel has raised his standard high ;
   And a peer his bribe hath ta'en."

For the peer there is an axe ; for the rebel there are
     racks ;
   For a yeoman there's a hempen string.
I heard a little bird singing in the sky ;—
" There are deaths for the low man, the middle, and
     the high,
   By the grace of our lord the King ! "

                      Mary Colborne-Veel.

CLXXIII.

The House We Build at Last.

   How small the house we build at last !
     How strangely altered is our pride ;
  One darkened room is all we ask,
     No garish light on any side ;
  One narrow bed for perfect rest,
  One bed—there is no other guest !

                         K

We build it safe, for use, not show
   (All our vain fancies are outworn),
The roof is very plain and low,
   We have no care for praise or scorn ;
We learn such perfect taste at last,
When all our vulgar pride is past !

We have no care of those who come,
   No fear that they will smile or jest
At our small solitary home,
   Or say that this, or that, were best ;
For in our city, each and all
Build very quietly and small.

We have no restless love for change,
   No wish to climb, no fear to fall ;
No craving for the new or strange,
   No rude, unseemly haste at all ;
We've learned the perfect grace of rest,
We've learned that silence is the best !

The storm may rave, the storm may cease,
   Or kingdoms sink, or kingdoms rise ;
It never breaks our perfect peace,
   Whate'er befalls beneath the skies ;
Our lowly house, and narrow land
Are safe from envy's cruel hand.

Ah, yes ! the home we build at last,
   Is better far than all the rest,
What, though the vanity is past !
   What, though we have no pleasant guest !
We have forgotten quite to weep,
And learned to be content with sleep.

                    Francis Sinclair.

CLXXIV.

Memento Mori.

THINK Thou, the Night shall come—
And on thy drifting senses steal the clang
Of Time's great gates behind thee, ere thou go
Into the shadows of the dark beyond !
Then with no terror, shalt thou slip thy hand
In the great angel Death's—as in a friend's—
And walk with him, barefooted, to the Dawn.

Amy Fowles.

CLXXV.

Cotswold Hills.

I SHALL die on Cotswold hills
    Where'er my body dies,
For space and time grow futile things
    As man's free spirit flies ;
One keen desire may touch the boon
    Denied to living eyes.

My last breath shall meet the breeze
    That blows o'er high, chill downs,
Where the slow-coming barley's gold
    Each rippling summit crowns ;
Or I shall tread the pleasant lanes
    That lead 'twixt little towns.

Fountain and swift-falling stream
    Shall greet my dying ears.
The brave stone cottages set firm
    Through centuries of years,
The English flowers, the English fields
    Win my last smiles and tears.

Cotswold slopes shall speak farewell
    In murmuring of bees,
In wafts of sweet-leaf'd eglantine
    Or fruitful apple-trees,
And so, content at last, my soul
    May wander on from these.

I shall die on Cotswold hills
    Where'er my body dies.
That moment, on the climbing road,
    A Cotsal school-child cries,
" Who passes yonder up our ways ?
    Look, what strange, glad, grey eyes ! "

Mary Colborne-Veel.

CLXXVI.

The Burial of Sir John McKenzie.

THEY played him home to the House of Stones,
    All the way, all the way,
To his grave in the sound of the winter sea.
    The sky was dour, the sky was gray.
They played him home with the cheiftain's dirge
Till the wail was wed to the rolling surge.
They played him home with a sorrowful will
To his grave at the foot of the Holy Hill ;
    And the pipes went mourning all the way.

Strong hands that had struck for right
   All the day, all the day,
Folded now in the dark of earth—
   The veiled dawn of the upper way !
Strong hands that struck with his
From days that were to the day that is
Carry him now from the house of woe
To ride the way the Chief must go ;
   And his peers went mourning all the way.

Son and brother at his right hand
   All the way, all the way !
And oh for them and oh for her
   Who stayed within, the dowie day !
Son and brother and near of kin
Go out with the Chief who never comes in !
And of all who loved him far and near
'Twas the nearest most that held him dear ;
   And his kin went mourning all the way.

The clan went on with the pipes before
   All the way, all the way ;
A wider clan than ever he knew
   Followed him home that dowie day.
And who were they of the wider clan ?—
The landless man and the No Man's man,
The man that lacked and the man unlearned,
The man that lived but as he earned ;
   And the clan went mourning all the way.

The heart of New Zealand went beside
   All the way, all the way,
To the resting-place of her Highland Chief :
   Much she thought she could not say.

He found her a land of many domains,
Maiden forest and fallow plains :
He left her a land of many homes,—
The pearl of the world, where the sea-wind roams ;
 And New Zealand went mourning all the way !

Jessie Mackay.

CLXXVII.

William Rolleston.

CLOSE his fair volume of true word and deed
For the still hour when sorrow is alone
With the beloved ; when the heart has grown
Less poignant for his parting, we shall need
His bland, sweet wisdom, sacrosanctest creed
Of truth omnipotent above all throne,
Or people, till the larger life be known
Wherefor he scattered oft the earliest seed.
Oh ! Godlike charity for the oppressed,
Clear spirit looking to the border goal
With eyes not politic, but shining far
With the upspringing rectitude of soul,
Be here with us, still striving, from thy rest,
Forget not in the glory of a star !

Hubert Church.

CLXXVIII.

The Gray Company.

Oh the gray, gray company
  Of the pallid dawn !
Oh the ghostly faces,
  Ashen-like and drawn !
The Lord's lone sentinels
  Dotted down the years—
The little gray company
  Before the pioneers !

Dreaming of Utopias
  Ere the time was ripe,
They awoke to scorning,
  The dungeon and the stripe.
Dreaming of millenniums
  In a world of wars,
They awoke to shudder
  At a flaming Mars.

Never was a Luther
  But a Huss was first,
A fountain unregarded
  In the primal thirst.
Never was a Newton
  Crowned and honoured well,
But first a lone Galileo
  Wasted in a cell.

In each other's faces
　　Looked the pioneers ;
Drank the wine of courage
　　All their battle years.
For their weary sowing
　　Through the world wide,
Green they saw the harvest
　　Ere the day they died.

But the gray, gray company
　　Stood every man alone
In the chilly dawnlight :
　　Scarcely had they known
Ere the day they perished
　　That their beacon-star
Was not glint of marshlight
　　In the shadows far.

The brave white witnesses
　　To the truth within
Took the dart of folly,
　　Took the jeer of sin.
Crying, " Follow, follow,
　　Back to Eden-gate ! "
They trod the Polar desert,
　　Met a desert fate.

Be laurel to the victor,
　　And roses to the fair,
And asphodel Elysian
　　Let the hero wear :

But lay the maiden lilies
   Upon their narrow biers—
The lone gray company
   Before the pioneers!

                Jessie Mackay.

CLXXIX.

My Father.

HE is old now,
And Time and Care have long ago
Covered his locks with winter's snow,
And lined his brow.

His step is slow,
Oft in his walk he stands to rest,
With folded arms upon his breast,
And head bent low.

His eyes are dim,
This world is fading from his sight,
But flower, and tree, and sun, and light,
Are naught to him.

The past is his,
And all day long his thoughts will roam,
And weave again in fancy's loom
Old memories.

At night I hear
His tottering footsteps cross the hall;
Slowly and solemnly they fall
Upon my ear.

                    K2

Some night I know
That I shall list for them in vain,
That I shall never go again,
To kiss his brow.

Perchance e'en now
The Angel beckons him away,
And I, O God ! would have him stay
With me below.

I cannot weep.
I watch him slipping from my side—
Gliding upon life's ebbing tide
To dreamless sleep.

But tears unshed
Scorch all the fibres of my heart.
There will be none to soothe the smart
When he is dead.

O God ! I cry,
Spare him to me ! He is my all !
Or bid thine Angel speed to call
Me too, to die !

Annie Murgatroyd.

CLXXX.

When the Sobbing is Over.

WHEN the sobbing is over, and Death
Comes kissing and stealing thy breath,
And the angel unlooseth the strings
    Of the brain, and its window, the eyes
(Where the soul, the great secret, hath lain),
    Thou shalt wonder with gladsome surprise.
        The secret of azuline gems,
        The wonder of world upon world,
        The secret of life and of joy,
The wonder of star upon star,
Where the beautiful shall be, and are ;
When Death cleaveth a pathway for Life
Where the beautified shall be, and are !

When the sobbing is over, and Death
Sets the seal of God on thy breath,
And thy soul (the great secret) is free
    From the trouble and sorrow and sin,
Thou shalt know all these beautiful things,
    In the shout that shall welcome thee in !
        The secret of bliss upon bliss—
        The " why " and the " therefore " of death,
        The secret of azuline gems,
The glory of meteor and star,
Where the beautiful shall be, and are !
Thou shalt know all the glories of life
Where the beautified shall be, and are !

W. R. Wills.

CLXXXI.

Song of the Drift Weed.

Here's to the home that was never, never ours !
Toast it full and fairly when the winter lowers.
Speak ye low, my merry men, sitting at your ease ;
Harken to the homeless Drift in the roaring seas !

Here's to the life we shall never live on earth !
Cut for us awry, awry ages ere the birth.
Set the teeth and meet it well, wind upon the shore ;
Like a lion, in the face look the Nevermore !

Here's to the love we were never let to win !
What of that ? a many shells have a pearl within ;
Some are mated with the gold in the light of day ;
Some are buried fathoms deep, in the seas away.

Here's to the selves we shall never, never be !
We're the drift of the world and the tangle of the sea.
It's far beyond the Pleiad, it's out beyond the sun
Where the rootless shall be rooted when the wander-
　　year is done !

Jessie Mackay.

CLXXXII.

Living Water.

I am a little desert pool, O Lord,
　　The rains of God descend but rarely here ;
　　And barren sands surround me far and near,
Save where a niggard circle of green sward
Grows, not ungrateful for the moisture poured
　　In rare and blessed hours of overflow.

And this is all, alas, I have to show—
So wide a waste, so small a precious hoard
Of living water.—Yet thou art my source ;
   I feel deep in my heart the sacred spring
That sends the mighty rivers on their course.
Let me be faithful to the impulse given,
   And though too weak to rise and flowing sing,
Let me reflect the calm and shining heaven.

Mary E. Richmond.

CLXXXIII.

Mary.

FROM her childhood flitting fancies came,
   Shapes of beauty, shapes of holy fear ;
   Gentle visions shining heavenly clear,
Ardent spirits formed of air and flame :

These made life a glory and a shame,
   Held her blind to duties small and near,
   Rapt beyond this rolling earthly sphere,
And her secret joys were chilled by blame.

But the Lord of Love, in human guise,
   Read His lowly servant's troubled heart,
Met with sympathy her pleading eyes ;

Saw the sorrow in her quiet face,
   Who had chosen first the better part ;
Bade them leave her listening in her place.

Mary E. Richmond.

CLXXXIV.

A Little Prayer.

My days are Thine, O Lord, assign
  To me a sphere of labour,
That I to Thee may faithful be
  And mindful of my neighbour.

My sins forgive, and let me live
  A life more pure and holy,
And if success my efforts bless,
  O Lord, then keep me lowly.

Dower me with strength to tread the length
  Of life's dim highway yonder,
More faith and grace to see Thy face
  Whene'er inclined to wander.

Give me a friend with whom to spend
  Life's golden hours in gladness,
A comrade, who remaineth true,
  Alike in joy or sadness.

A little bread, a roof, a bed,
  And each new morn a blessing,
Is all I ask from week to week—
  These wants I come confessing.   Amen.

W. Francis Chambers.

CLXXXV.

Constraint.

I HEARD a voice crying unto me,
And I answered, " Yea, Lord."
And it spoke again saying,
" Knowest thou me ? "
And I answered, " Yea, Lord."
And the voice spoke again, saying :
" Upon those that know is laid the burden ;
Arise, shine, for your light is come."
And I made answer, " O Lord, I am afraid."
And the voice ceased.
I rose up and turned away,
Moving along the well-worn path
To my own home.
But the ground was all stained
As with the steps of feet that bled ;
And I knew Who was before me,
Knew the love and the sorrow ;
And fear fell from me like a garment,
And I girt my robes about me,
And fled after Him—whither I could not tell ;
Only it was the way that He had gone.

Mary E. Richmond.

CLXXXVI.

The Judgment.

To thunder-sounds last night I had a dream
  Of going up before God's Judgment Seat,
  Along a great and wide gold-paven street,
And by the fount that feeds the crystal stream ;
On dome and turret the red lightning's gleam
  Made vengeful lights, and my reluctant feet
  Fain would have stayed where angels come and meet
World-weary ones that Love and Death redeem.

No throng of spirits filled the Judgment Hall,
  No king in purple and in gold array,
But a pale shape that surely might appal,
  Seraph or demon, in a garment gray,
Sate there to judge :   'Twas my own soul, and all
  The Heaven resounded with the Judgment Day.

D. M. Ross.

CLXXXVII.

Prelude to " The Nazarene."

I WILL not have his human story dimmed
And shadowed over by his divinity.
He was of us, all human, brother, friend ;
He strove, was vanquished, strove and won—a Man.

About his path no cloud of angels hung,
Legions and legions watching him ; no hand
Lifted him up above his sufferings.
He walked not on the clouds, but here with us,

Living obscurely on this common earth
His common life.   The sweat upon his brow
Was bitter human sweat ; the heart we pierced,
A heart that long had learnt the lonely way
That breaking hearts must go.

                       And at the end

This is his chiefest glory—that he rose
No higher than the cross we built for him !

Oh that the world might know him as he was—
The kindly teacher, the sweet, patient man,
One of our human family, Mary's son !

I cannot know the Christ ; the time is late,
And he that walked among us, sore at heart,
Has faded from us, merged into a God.

The sweet familiar Nazarene is lost
Beneath the waving of fine priestly hands ;
His tender, troubled face looks dimly out
Across the incense-smoke ; I cannot hear
His quiet tones beneath the breathless throb
Of vast, sonorous organs ; and the bruised
And wounded body we would weep upon
Is covered from our pitying gaze with stiff
And costly vestments ; he is buried deep
In piles of carven stone, and lies forgotten
Beneath the triumph of cloud-questing spires.

His simple kindliness and frequent smile—
The sweet humanity that was the Christ—
Is frightened by the stillness and the awe,
And drowned in the vast hush of solemn aisles.
The light strays feebly through the rich-hued panes ;

I cannot recognize the Man who loved
The sun and all the simple sunny things.
I put my hands out blindly for a breast
Of close, familiar comfort—and I feel
The cold, smooth pavement and the carven stone !

And when among the long-dead centuries
I seek the Man, I cannot see him clear ;
For he is hidden by a cloud of wings,
Or blinds me, radiant, an effulgent God !

His body was not rapt in splendour up,
But somewhere with us lies, his ashes sealed
In some long-fallen tomb : not reft away,
Somewhere they build up soil and seed and soul.
Or somewhere they are blown about the world,
Part of the green of grass, the blue of sky,
Helping the herb—as all of us must help—
Woven and mixed within all growing things.

Oh that the world might know him as he was—
One of our human family, Mary's son !

Arthur H. Adams.

CLXXXVIII.

Rangiora.

THE land has no antiquity
　　(Said the little voice in my head.)
After all it has no history....
　　(No history, it said.)

I was riding along by Rangiora,
And considering how through endless blue August days
I had ridden from village to village
In the holy land of England ;
And every fold in the ground,
And every turn in the road
Was full of remembrances and histories.
And that is why the voice said, No history,
No history it said.

But what is history ?
So I looked at the sacred fields of harvest
Consecrated by the labour of man and the blessing of
    heaven,
And strove to see their story.

And I saw the swamp and the bush of long ago
And the wild brown marsh birds flying to and fro,
The bittern and the heron, and the owl,
And all the clutter of screaming river-fowl,
As man rides into the silent sanctuaries
And pools of the wood, paddling his own canoe,
To build his hut, and plant the kumara,
And little wild children playing in the trees.

So the Maori heads the procession,
That consecrates this land with labour and blood.
Then come the white men with the axe and gun,
And the birds are killed, and the trees lie low in the sun,
And the ground is cleared and stubbed and burned and
    drained ;
And each descending day
Is another chapter in history,
And another acre gained.

And the long march goes on :
They come with harrow and plough : with pick and
    spade they come,
No music with their march, no bugle and no drum,
No colours swinging high, no clapping, and no cry,
No ribbons and streamers gay.

They march through glory of sunny summer days,
Through streams of pouring rain,
Through frosts that bind the plain.
With horse and dog they ride uneven ways ;
By pain they attain,
And labour and agony.

This is the high procession that I saw
(And would love to draw)
Wind round the paddocks by the gorse fence edge,
Blessing the boundary hedge,
And consecrating it with sweat and blood.
Who made that poplar grove ?
And drew those lines of oaks
That stiffly hide the little house of wood,
Whose hearthfire dimly smokes
A cloudy blue ?

I crept up, too,
And peeped in at the window that I might see
What lovely mystery
Was planted there,
Worth so much agony
And guarded with such care.

And there I saw a mother mild,
And in her lap a little child,
With the loveliness that Mary wore
In the stable of Bethlehem.
And this most lowly mystery
Is the end of every history
That every man shall come to adore
In the stable of Bethlehem.

Philip Carrington.

CLXXXIX.

To L.H.B. (1894-1915).

LAST night for the first time since you were dead
I walked with you, my brother, in a dream.
We were at home again beside the stream
Fringed with tall berry bushes, white and red.
" Don't touch them : they are poisonous," I said.
But your hand hovered, and I saw a beam
Of strange, bright laughter flying round your head,
And as you stooped I saw the berries gleam.
" Don't you remember ?   We called them Dead Man's
        Bread ! "
    I woke and heard the wind moan and the roar
Of the dark water tumbling on the shore.
Where—where is the path of my dream for my eager
        feet ?
By the remembered stream my brother stands
Waiting for me with berries in his hands....
    " These are my body.   Sister, take and eat."

Katharine Mansfield.

CXC.

The White Peril.

Up from the Nethermost Sea ;
*   Pallid ; with poisonous breath,*
Creeps God's terrible mystery
*   Death !*

MENACE of battle ?   To us ?   To children of war-worn
    men !
Sons of the grey-wolf Briton, cubs from the sea-wolf's
    den !
War would they have ?   Then we answer where sea-
    ward the battery flames ;
Shake out the rags of the fighting-flags and into the
    Game of Games !

Menace of Germany ?   Nay.   Come they as foes or as
    kin,
Grip o' the hand or grip o' the throat shall welcome the
    strangers in ;
Latin or Slav or Teuton, not to the beat of the Drum,
Not from the men of the Failing Broods will utter des-
    truction come.

Menace of Asia ?   Nay.   Over the Orient Sea
Rank upon rank of pitiless eyes watch us unceasingly ;
Patient, stolid, immutable ; quiet as passionless Fate,
Why should they leap at our rifles' mouths who have
    only to crouch and wait ?

Peril is here ! is here ! Here in the Childless Land
Life sits high in the Chair of Fools, twisting her ropes
    of sand ;
Here the lisping of babies and cooing of mothers cease ;
Here the Man and the Woman fail, and only the flocks
    increase.

Axes may bite in the forest, Science harness the streams,
Railway and dock be builded—all in a Land of Dreams !
Sunk in spiritual torpor ye flout these words of the wise,
" Only to music of children's songs shall the walls of a
    Nation rise."

Sleep, my brothers, and dream that ye gather the gold
    and the corn ;
Alien hands will hold your lands and scatter your
    graves in scorn ;
Blind to the Open Vision, ye see not in coming years
Dogs of the Tartar gnaw to dust the bones of the
    Pioneers.

Up from the Nethermost Sea ;
    Pallid ; with poisonous breath,
Creeps God's terrible mystery
    Death !

Edward Tregear.

CXCI.

A Temple Service.

(Ordained in Israel after the deliverance from Moab.)

PRIESTS.

THE days were drawn towards the sun,
  Kissed every one,
By lips red-ripe with summer sweet,
  From brow to feet.

Dawn's cold pale forehead with the black
  Night-hair pushed back,
Flushed feet of eve, that walk the west,
  Were caught and pressed.

PEOPLE.

Yet ere the months had failed of flower,
  Their branch of time
Grew heavy with a ripening hour,
  God's plant of prime.

More precious than the whitening wheat,
  Or swollen fig ;
Sweeter than palm fruit peeled to eat,
  Or grapes grown big.

PRIESTS.

Made-music for the harps we string,
  The silver ring
Of beaten cymbals which we raise
  On feasting days,

And on the lips of sweetest singers,
      Between the fingers
Of those that pluck at silver wires
      Of writhen lyres.

PEOPLE.

A psalm upon the psalteries,
    On shawms a song,
Upon the horns great harmonies,
    Blown loud and long ;

A writing for the scrolls of scribes,
    The graven gates
That tell the triumphs of the tribes
    On brazen plates.

PRIESTS.

Wherefore the heavy hearts and sad
      Be grown all glad,
And rainbow light in eyes yet rimmed
      By grief that dimmed.

Wherefore the mouth by mourning mute,
      The feeble foot,
Hath joy in it as meat and bread,
      Is strong of tread.

PEOPLE.

In garden ground the summer burns,
    Not yet grown old,
And on the corn whose colour turns
    From green to gold ;

But harvest men, before they make
  The sickle sharp,
Go up to keep the day's sweet sake
  With heart and harp.

PRIESTS.

It falls within the twofold time :
      The youngest prime
Of fruit, the latest looks of flowers,
      Are on its hours.

And blossoms sweet through loosening leaves,
      And early sheaves,
Green gathered from the growing wheat,
      Are offerings meet.

PEOPLE.

To lift up the slant scale of sin,
  And weigh at last
With righteous recompense cast in,
  Present with past,

The pleasant paths beneath our feet
  Were broken up ;
We tasted through the foam of sweet,
  A bitter cup.

PRIESTS.

" Because your hearts are waxen dead,"
      The Lord God said,
" And in your ears my name sounds cold,
      My name of old,

" I lift a sword upon the land ;
  A heavy hand
Between you and your sins falls keen
  To scourge you clean."

PEOPLE.

Was it so sweet from God to hide
  In garden ways,
The women large-lipped and long-eyed,
  What was their face ?

Were they so gracious in their groves,
  The lords of stone,
Or were their damsels dear with loves
  Beyond our own ?

PRIESTS.

The well-graved images which ye
  Were pleased to see,
Deeming gods, clear of face and fair
  Of form, were there ;

Gods gazed upon and drawn so near,
  Who could not hear,
Were they as He unseen and far
  In whom we are ?

PEOPLE.

The wanton women scorning stealth,
  Their lust confessed,
Spendthrift of red coin and white wealth,
  Of mouth and breast ;

Soft sin-flowers leaving poison pods
    For bitter birth,
Ungirdled girls and garden-gods,
    Were they well worth ?

PRIESTS.

Yea, what were all light-clothen charms,
        And stretched-out arms,
By the pure hearts from out you failed,
        Your virgins veiled ?

The flowery rods at first that beat
        So light and sweet,
Their flowers fell off from them yet fresh,
        Thorns tore the flesh.

PEOPLE.

" *Our gods are great,*" *the false priests said ;*
   " *For their fierce joys*
The fire must flow about the head
    Of girls and boys."

 Prone 'neath their women's soft queen-hood,
    Their lord's kingship
Smote off the silken servitude
    With bloody whip.

PRIESTS.

" Have ye a garland for your head ? "
        The wise God said.
" Lo ! here a fetter for your feet,
        It is but meet.

" For strangers ye My laws forsake,
   Their yokes to take ;
Think ye to choose the light and small
   Nor wear them all ? "

PEOPLE.

Our hosts were broken in the wars,
  And faint of heart
Fled home, and from his shut house-doors
  None durst depart.

Then were we aliens in our streets
  And father's fields,
Dogs to be glad of morsel meats
  A master yields.

PRIESTS.

Their captains chose them slaves at will
   To toil and till,
And princes for their serving men,
   By five and ten.

And spoused maidens for their bed,
   Cast out unwed
To be the sport of lewd women,
   And mock of men.

PEOPLE.

And so the time went heavily
  For years eighteen,
And God's face, which we sought to see,
  It was not seen.

The seasons moved from frost to flower,
  From flower to fruit,
But all the echoes of their power
  Were lost and mute.

PRIESTS.

But He who sits above the years
          He told our tears ;
He who before did count our crime
          In His good time,

From where He ruled, ordained a deed,
          To help our need,
And show the heathen, Israel
          Was yet loved well.

PEOPLE.

Under their king, even where he sat,
  Girt round with sin,
As with a garment, foul and fat,
  Without, within.

There, in his builded pleasant place,
  His windowed room,
That curtained out the summer days,
  Was sent a doom.

PRIESTS.

A secret message from the Lord,—
          Was not the sword
Of swift Ehud the pen of it ?
          The scribe was fit.

He wrote it where it might be read,
　　Wrote it and fled ;
We kept the fords and slew them, till
　　None were to kill.

PEOPLE.

A day among the days is thus
　　A feast ; there is
A man of all the tribes o'er us
　　A judge for this.

The day with service comes and parts,
　　And sacrifice ;
And in his hand are all our hearts
　　Held sceptre-wise.

Frederick Napier Broome.

CXCII.

L'Envoi.

So over, all over : the whistle peals " Time ! "
The field lies bare to the last of the light.
Too late to tell what you might have done ;
The goal is kicked, and a stronger has won.
To you is only the glow of the fight ;
To you is only the soreness and grime.

What matter, so long as you played the game ?
What matter, provided you filled your place,
And took the fall, the kick, the blow,
And tackled the foeman clean and low—
Blind sun in your eyes, wet wind in your face—
What matter, so met ye the luck as it came ?

Seaforth Mackenzie.

NOTES

***

To One in England (p. 3).—*Ngaio*: a handsome native shrub or small tree, with glossy leaves and pink spotted flowers.

The Night-watch of the "Charlotte Jane" (p. 4).—The *Charlotte Jane* was one of the four ships which brought the first emigrants to Canterbury. The author of the poem was the first Superintendent of the Province, and virtually the first Premier of New Zealand.

The Battle of the Free (p. 7).—These spirited verses, which have since proved prophetic, were written at the time of the Crimean war.

Early Days (p. 13).—*Kaka*: bush parrot. *Fossick*: hunt about. *Lollies*: sweetmeats. *Manuka*: a New Zealand shrub with small, aromatic, tea-like leaves.

For Love of Appin (p. 19).—The people of Appin, evicted and deported to America in the eighteenth century, wailed and sang "Lochaber no more" long after they put out to sea. It is said that the elder men never smiled again, lest they should be thought disloyal to Scotland.

The Dwellings of our Dead (p. 21).—*Tui*: the tui, sometimes called the mocking-bird, and also known as the parson bird from the little tuft of white feathers that sticks out from its throat, contrasting with its dark plumage, is a bird larger and more shapely than the blackbird. "Its plumage," says one vivid writer, "is lustrous black, irradiated with green hues, and pencilled with silver grey, and it displays a white throat-tuft for its clerical bands. It can sing, but seldom will, and it preserves its voice for mocking others. Darting through some low scrub to the topmost twig of the tallest tree, it commences roaring forth a variety of strange notes, with such changes of voice and volume of tone as to claim the instant attention of the forest." *Toi*: a New Zealand pampas grass. *Bush*: the name always given to the New Zealand Forest.

A Leave-taking (p. 28).—*Bell-bird* (or *Makomako*) : the beauty of the bell-bird's song delighted Captain Cook, who heard it when his ship was lying about a quarter of a mile from the shore. " And in the morning," he says, " we were wakened by the singing of the birds. The number was incredible, and they seemed to strain their throats in emulation of each other. This wild melody was infinitely superior to any that we have ever heard, of the same kind ; it seemed to be like small bells, most exquisitely tuned ; and perhaps the distance and the water between might be no small advantage to the sound."

In London (p. 35).—*Weka* : the flightless native woodhen.

A New Zealand Picture (p. 51).—*Otaki* : a river in the North Island flowing into Cook Strait.

Tauranga (p. 52).—*Pa* : a Maori fortified village.

The Passing of the Forest (p. 56).—*Tane* : the god of trees.

In the Moonlight (p. 75).—" *The trappers are out on the hills to-night* " : the reference is to the rabbit-killing. The rabbit, introduced into New Zealand for purposes of sport, is now chiefly a pest. The export of skins, however, forms one of the minor industries of the country.

Arlington (p. 81).—*Cockatoos* : small runholders.

The Old Place (p. 82).—*Tauhinu* : an aromatic shrub infesting poor soil. *Karaka* : a bush tree with shining dark-green foliage.

The Whare (p. 84).—*Whare* : Maori name for a house or shelter.

The Blind, Obedient Dead (p. 91).—A curious memorial of the Boer war is recorded from Surrey. At Burstaw, in that county, a drinking trough and fountain have been erected by a local personage in memory of four hundred thousand horses killed and wounded during the South African War, from 1899 to 1902, " in a cause of which they knew nothing."—Daily Paper.

The Mountain Spirit (p. 111).—*Aorangi* (cloud-piercer) is the Maori name of Mount Cook, in the Southern Alps, the highest peak in New Zealand. *Kea* : a native bird of the parrot family.

Onawe (p. 112).—*Onawe* is a small peninsula in Akaroa harbour, which was fortified by the Maoris of Canterbury for their last stand against the terrible North Island chief, Te Rauparaha, early in the last century. The fortress, which appeared almost impregnable, was captured by a stratagem, and a fearful slaughter took place. Onawe had previously been held sacred as the home of the spirit (or *atua*) of the wind, who took his flight from the place, and prophesied the downfall of the Southern Maoris, in revenge for the sacrilegious discharge of a musket near his immemorial abode. *Pakeha* : white man, stranger. *Haka* : war-dance. *Rangitiras* : chieftains. *Tenakoe* : a word of greeting.

The Four Queens (p. 118).—*Eden*: Mount Eden, one of the chief suburbs of Auckland.

The River Avon (p. 120).—The Avon is the river on which Christ-church stands. It was really named after a Scottish stream by the Deans brothers, who settled near its banks about ten years before the arrival of the main body of Canterbury colonists.

The City from the Hills (p. 124).—Christchurch, which is also referred to in the following poem.

Akaroa (p. 127).—Akaroa was originally a French settlement, formed in 1840. It was also a great port of whalers. *Try-pot*: the huge pots in which the oil was tried out.

Te Raupo (p. 135).—The raupo, or New Zealand bulrush. *Kakino*: treacherous.

To the Makomako (p. 140).—See note to " A Leave-taking."

Ti-trees and the Kukupa (p. 142).—*Kukupa*: wood-pigeon.

The Riro-riro (p. 143).—The grey warbler, one of the sweetest of New Zealand singing birds.

New Zealand (p. 153).—*Tangaroa*: the Maori God of the sea. *Maui*: the Polynesian Hercules, with a certain spice of Mercury, also of Prometheus. He clipped the wings of the sun, stole fire from the Fire Goddess, fished up New Zealand from the sea, and all but conquered the Goddess of Death. *Te Ika*; the fish (Te Ika a Maui is the fish of Maui, the Maori name properly for the North Island only of New Zealand, but often for the whole country).

The Coming of Te Rauparaha (p. 156).—*Te Rauparaha*, sometimes not unfitly called the Maori Napoleon, was the chief of the Ngatitoa tribe, in the southern part of the North Island. Arming his followers with muskets, he seized and fortified the island of Kapiti, whence he made daring incursions against the tribes of the mainland. The strong *pah* of Kaiapohia, in Canterbury, having incurred his hostility, he led an expedition against it, in about the year 1829, and took the fortress after a six month's siege. The remnant of the Canterbury Maoris who remained to oppose him were defeated at Onawe, as narrated in the note to " Onawe " (p. 112). Subsequently Te Rauparaha was the constant terror of the first settlers at Wellington. His son became a zealous missionary to the tribes the father had de-vastated. *Hapu*: sub-tribe. *Mere*: a stone club. *Pah*: fortified village. *Mana*: prestige, reputation. *Te Reinga*: the " leaping place " of souls ; at the extreme north of New Zealand, whence they entered into the lower world.

The March of Te Rauparaha (p. 163).—*Kapai* : a word of approbation.

The Lament for Mōrēré (p. 170).—The original of Tamati Honé's lament for his sons and tribesmen killed in the vain attack on Sentry Hill Redoubt, Te Mōrēré, in Taranaki, in 1864, was recited to the translator by Whareaitu and by Te Kahu-Pukoro, Tamati's grandson. Te Kahu himself was wounded there, on the fatal glacis of Sentry Hill in 1864, when the rifles of the British Garrison poured a shower of death on the charging Hauhau fanatics. To-day the dirge is sung at *tangis*, or weeping-parties, in the villages of the Ngati-Ruanui and Nga-Ruahine on the Waimate Plains and from Patea to the foot of Taranaki Mountain. Tiopira, mentioned in the poem, was the father of Te Kahu-Pukoro. Whole families fell in this desperate attempt to assault a strong British post in broad daylight.

The Noosing of the Sun-God (p. 173).—One old Maori tradition says that Maui, one of the demi-gods, when he strove to bind the swift-rushing sun, could not prevail till he made a rope of his sister Ina's hair. *Tiraha, Te Ra* : Slower, O Sun. *Rangi* : the sky. *Po* : the Maori underworld. *Eyes of the Kings* : the Maoris believed that on the death of very famous chiefs their eyes became stars.

Fairyland (p. 216).—*Parson bird* (or *tui*) : see note on " The Dwellings of our Dead " (p. 21).

The Home Coming (p. 230).—In June, 1906, Richard John Seddon, who had been Prime Minister for thirteen years, and who was then at the height of his fame and power and a great national figure, embarked for New Zealand after a visit to Australia. He died suddenly on the evening of his sailing. A week later his body was brought home across the Tasman Sea for burial.

To Sir George Grey (p. 230).— *Sir George Grey* was Governor of New Zealand for terms of several years immediately before and after his governorship of Cape Colony. At a later period he was Superintendent of the province of Auckland, one of the representatives of Auckland city in Parliament, and for two years Premier of the Colony.

Nausicaa (p. 235).—*Nausicaa* was the daughter of Alcinous, King of Phæacia, an island in the Ionian Sea. She first met Ulysses, who had been shipwrecked on the shores of the island, while she was busy with her maidens washing her father's garments by the sea. *Bridegroom* : according to Aristotle this was Telemachus, son of Ulysses.

The Burial of Sir John McKenzie (p. 260).— *John McKenzie*, a typical Highland shepherd who emigrated to Otago in 1860, was for some years Minister of Lands, and is chiefly remembered for his lands for settlement policy, referred to in the poem.

William Rolleston (p. 262).—*William Rolleston*, born in 1831, was a member of a Commission which framed the educational system of Canterbury. Afterwards he was for eight years Superintendent of that province, and he also held various portfolios in different colonial governments.

On the Pronunciation of Maori Words.

Every vowel in Maori words is pronounced separately (*Whare*, *Petone*), and receives the same quality as in Italian. The stress usually falls on the first and alternative syllables. (But *Rauparaha* is accented on the first and final syllables). *Ng* is nasal. Final vowels are sometimes voiceless.

INDEX OF AUTHORS
AND BIBLIOGRAPHICAL REFERENCE

Thanks are due to the authors, publishers, and owners of copyright mentioned below—as many as we have been able to trace—for permission to use the verses referred to against their names. Verses which have been published more than once are referred to their first appearance in an independent volume by their author ; in the absence of such a volume, to their place of first publication, as far as is known. The references are to the numbers of the pieces.

ADAMS, ARTHUR H.—*Maoriland, and Other Verses.* Sydney : The *Bulletin* Newspaper Company Limited, 1899. (ix, xii, lxx, xciv, cxxiii). *London Streets* (cliv). *The Nazarene : A Study of a Man.* London : Philip Wellby, 1902. (clxxxvii).

ALLISON, HENRY.—cxlii, cxliii, cxlv, clxiii, clxiv.

ANDERSEN, JOHANNES C.— *Songs Unsung.* Christchurch : Whitcombe and Tombs Limited, 1903. (xxxiv, lxxxvii, lxxxviii, cxxi, cxxxviii).

AUGUST, S. G.— *Stewart Island Verses and Others,* by Southerner, Invercargill, 1923. Craft Agency Coy. (xxiii).

BARR, JOHN, of Craigilee.—*Poems and Songs, Descriptive and Satirical.* Edinburgh : John Greig and Son, 1861. (cvii, cviii, cx).

BATHGATE, ALEXANDER.—*Far South Fancies.* London : Griffith, Farran, Okeden and Welsh, N.D., 1889. (xxxii, lxxxvi, cxxxvi).

BAUGHAN, B. E.— *Reuben, and Other Poems.* Westminster : Archibald Constable and Company, 1903. (xliv). *Shingle Short, and Other Verses.* Christchurch : Whitcombe and Tombs Limited. (vi, xliv, xciii). *Poems from the Port Hills.* Christchurch : Whitcombe and Tombs Limited. (cxli).

BEAGLEHOLE, J. C.—(clxii).

BOWDEN, BOYCE.—*Wellington Verses.* Wellington : Whitcombe and Tombs Limited, 1917. (lxxxi).

BOWEN, CHARLES C.—*Poems.* Christchurch : Union Office, 1861. (iv, v).

BRACKEN, THOMAS.—*Lays of the Land of the Maori and Moa.* London : Sampson Low, Marston, Searle and Rivington, 1884. (xcv, cxxix, cli, clxviii).

THE BOOK OF CANTERBURY RHYMES. Christchurch: Ward and Reeves, 1866. (iii).

CANTERBURY RHYMES. Second Edition. Edited by W. P. Reeves. Christchurch: *The Lyttelton Times* Company Limited, 1883. (xi).

THE JUBILEE BOOK OF CANTERBURY RHYMES. Edited by O. T. J. Alpers. Christchurch: Whitcombe and Tombs Limited, 1900. (lxiii, lxix, cxvi, clxiii).

COLLEGE RHYMES. Edited by O. T. J. Alpers and others. Christchurch: Whitcombe and Tombs Limited, 1923. (lxxviii, clxxviii).

CHAMBERS'S JOURNAL, Edinburgh. (xxxix, lxii, cli).

THE BULLETIN, Sydney. (xlviii, xlix, lvii, lviii, lix, lxvii, lxviii, cxi). Besides the pieces taken directly from *The Bulletin*, and all the verse from *Maoriland, and Other Verses*, and *The West Wind*, the following pieces, mentioned elsewhere as republished by their authors, also appear in this book by permission of *The Bulletin* Newspaper Company Limited, the owners of the copyright :—(lxiv, cxxx, cxxxii, clx).

THE CANTERBURY COLLEGE REVIEW, Christchurch. (clix).

GLEANINGS FROM AUSTRALASIAN VERSE. Gathered by Mary E. Wilkinson. Melbourne: Whitcombe and Tombs Limited. (cxvii).

THE HUIA, Auckland. (cxxii).

THE MONTHLY REVIEW, London. (x).

THE NEW ZEALAND ILLUSTRATED MAGAZINE, Auckland. (xix, xxxi, xxxvii, cxx, cxlii, cxliii, cxlv).

NEW ZEALAND LIFE AND FOREST MAGAZINE, Wellington. (xxviii).

NEW ZEALAND SELECT JOURNAL. (cxxxviii).

NEW ZEALAND VERSE (First Edition). (xlv, lxxi, xcviii, cxlii, cxlix).

THE OTAGO WITNESS, Dunedin. (xli, xcix, cxxxiv, cxxxv, cl, xxviii).

THE SPIKE, OR VICTORIA COLLEGE REVIEW, Wellington. (lii, cxliv, clxii, cxcii).

THE SUN, Christchurch. (cxxxix, clxvi).

THE TRIAD, Dunedin. (xxxv).

THE WEEKLY PRESS, Christchurch. (cxxvii).

VICTORIAN REVIEW, Melbourne. (cxlvi).

YOUNG AUSTRALIA, Sydney. (xcii).

We believe the following pieces to be published now for the first time : xxii, lxxx, lxxxix, xcviii.

Index of First Lines